I0901909

MATT'S ST. LOUIS FOOD STORY

Bars, Restaurants, Shops, and Other Purveyors

BY MATT SORRELL

REEDY PRESS

DEDICATION

To my wife, Beth, who always has my six.

Copyright © 2025 by Reedy Press, LLC
Reedy Press
PO Box 5131
St. Louis, MO 63139, USA
reedypress.com

No part of this publication may be reproduced or transmitted in any form or by any means, electronic or mechanical, including photocopy, recording, or any information storage and retrieval system, without permission in writing from the publisher.

Permissions may be sought directly from Reedy Press at the above mailing address or via our website at reedypress.com.

Library of Congress Control Number: 2025942436

ISBN: 9781681066196

Cover illustration by Dan Zettwoch

Design by Rich Roden

Back cover image (right) courtesy Mabel Suen

Unless otherwise noted, all photos are courtesy of the author or believed to be in the public domain.

Printed in Canada
25 26 27 28 29 5 4 3 2 1

We (the publisher and the author) have done our best to provide the most accurate information available when this book was completed. However, we make no warranty, guarantee, or promise about the accuracy, completeness, or currency of the information provided, and we expressly disclaim all warranties, express or implied. Please note that attractions, company names, addresses, websites, and phone numbers are subject to change or closure, and this is outside of our control. We are not responsible for any loss, damage, injury, or inconvenience that may occur due to the use of this book. When exploring new destinations, please do your homework before you go. You are responsible for your own safety and health when using this book.

CONTENTS

INTRODUCTION

St. Louis has an abundance of deliciousness within its borders. We might be on the smallish side as far as major metropolitan areas go, but our culinary offerings dwarf those of much more populous locales. In the more than 20 years that I've been writing about the STL food and drink scene and working in the food service industry here, I've noticed that way too many people, both in and out of town, don't appreciate this fact. With *Matt's St. Louis Food Story*, I hope to rectify this by making locals aware of what they're missing in their own backyard while allowing outsiders looking in an opportunity to understand why St. Louis's gastronomical prowess is not to be denied.

St. Louis food offerings really run the gamut. There's something for every taste and flavorful inclination here. Establishments like Crown Candy Kitchen, Gioia's Deli, and Failoni's opened their doors while the country was still in the throes of the First World War and continue to honor the traditions they sprang from. Meanwhile, cutting-edge eateries like Neon Greens, with its plant-based focus and on-site hydroponic farm, and multirestaurant concepts like City Foundry Food Hall reimagine the idea of dining out in the 21st century. Fine dining spots like Bistro La Floraison share favored status with neighborhood joints like Iowa Buffet. Our rich variety of immigrant communities is represented by markets and restaurants galore, representing everywhere from Asia to Africa.

While this book is populated with a cross-section of some of the top-tier places in town, it's by no means a greatest hits collection or a best-of list. Trying to rank a city's worth of bars, restaurants, purveyors, and producers is the ultimate fool's errand. Instead, the places and products listed on these pages, icons and newcomers alike, represent a tasty map of the area that serves as a point of entry for further explorations of the cuisines, neighborhoods, and cultures that make St. Louis City and County great.

The Whiskey Ring
Courtesy of Nate Burrell

ACKNOWLEDGMENTS

I'd like to thank the Reedy Press team for both the opportunity to tell the stories within these pages and for helping me bring them to life. Thanks as well to all the publications I've been privileged to write for over the years for providing me a place to develop my voice and for fostering my interest in the food and drink scene in St. Louis. Finally, I want to express my gratitude to all of the folks who work hard every day to keep us fed. It's a tough, thankless gig, but know that you are seen and valued. Cheers to you all.

BARS

THE HIDEAWAY

5900 Arsenal St. | 314.645.8822 | thehideawaystl.com

A neighborhood bar is so much more than a just a place to grab a drink. It's a refuge from the day-to-day, where a weary worker bee can duck in and check out for a while. It provides a space where folks can sit back and silently people-watch or lean in and engage in conversations that run the gamut from the latest celebrity saga to the numerous failings of our political representatives. It's a spot to watch the game, listen to music (live or otherwise), and engage with a unique cross section of the community on one's own terms.

Established in 1954, the Hideaway is all of these things and more. It's not just a watering hole, though you can surely get a quality, reasonable-priced beverage there. From the orange shag carpeting that adorns the front of the bar to the pair of misty and mysterious portraits of buxom young women that watch over the bottles on the back bar, the Hideaway has its own unique feel that transcends trends. On a typical night, guests can play a game or two of darts or pet some of the numerous dogs that regularly drop in with their owners. As the sign out front says, the Hideaway is also a piano bar and is well known around town for raucous weekly sing-alongs. It's a favorite karaoke destination for those who want to unleash their inner diva. Once a month customers can try their hand at meat bingo for the chance to take home some prime cuts.

All of these disparate elements meld together and create a welcoming vibe

that permeates the Hideaway and makes even first-timers feel like regulars. Stop in, belly up to the bar, and let the rest of the world roll on by.

IOWA BUFFET

2727 Winnebago St. | 314.776.8000

Located at the confluence of Iowa Avenue and Winnebago Street in Dutchtown, Iowa Buffet is the very definition of a corner dive bar. The old-school Budweiser neon sign over the door hints at the bar's bona fides as a classic neighborhood drinking establishment, a vibe backed up inside by the tattered barstools and the ghost scent of cigarettes past. Unfortunately, you might run into some sock hat hipsters and selfie-taking scenesters when you visit, but they'll be easily outnumbered by the everyday folks who find refuge from the daily grind here amid the cheap wood paneling and exposed ductwork.

The food menu is replete with bar favorites like wings, fried pickle chips, onion rings, and jalapeño poppers. My advice is to take advantage of the burgers, like the Duke of Iowa, topped with pub cheese, bacon jam, and chili sauce. All burgers are cooked in the ancient broiler situated behind the bar, in full view of God and everyone. Grill fans, Saturdays at Iowa Buffet mean barbecue, from ribs and pork steaks to brats, served with two sides and dessert. Of course, there's always plenty of frosty cold beer and shots of mid-tier booze to wash it all down.

The cozy confines of Iowa Buffet make it almost impossible not to be entertained by your fellow barflies. The last time I bellied up to the bar I was privy to a pretty intense *King of the Hill* trivia deep dive at the table behind me. Judging from the bucket of empty Buds on the table, it had been a long fight, the winner uncertain. For more professional entertainment options, Iowa Buffet also hosts periodic bouts of live music, and there's always the jukebox to fall back on.

PLANTER'S HOUSE

1000 Mississippi Ave. | 314.696.2603 | plantershousestl.com

Perhaps no spot in St. Louis embodies the "what's old is new" ethos better than Planter's House. Located in the historic Lafayette Square neighborhood, Planter's House takes its name from the bar at the Planter's Hotel, which served thirsty St. Louisans from 1817 to 1922 and where OG celebrity bartender Jerry Thomas once worked.

The bar boasts one of the largest selections of private-barrel spirits in the US along with a list of cocktails made with said spirits and an ever-evolving roster of seasonal libations and cocktails on tap. I've been lucky enough to work behind this bar, and believe me, the staff can replicate most any cocktail, classic or otherwise. To accompany the drinks, the Planter's kitchen serves up a variety of comfort dishes with a French-bistro vibe.

Food and drink aside, Planter's House has atmosphere to spare. It's located in what was originally two buildings, both dating from the latter half of the 19th century. The main dining room has a soaring ceiling of curved wood that evokes the prow of a ship and a trio of chandeliers from the 1920s that once illuminated the old City of St. Louis police station. The adjacent Bullock Room is named after bartender Tom Bullock, famous for being the first African American to write a cocktail recipe book, who plied his trade at the St. Louis Country Club in the early part of the 20th century.

Courtesy of Mabel Suen

Courtesy of Greg Rannells

For all you Christmas fans, during the holiday season Planter's House puts regular service on hold and transforms into Sippin' Santa, a tiki-esque experience that's one of the most popular Christmas-themed cocktail pop-ups in town.

VENICE CAFE

1903 Pestalozzi St. | 314.772.5994 | thevenicecafe.com

Part art installation, part music venue, part watering hole, the Venice Cafe has been a cornerstone of the St. Louis community since 1988, when owner Jeff Lockheed first opened the space to the public.

The building, located in Benton Park in the shadow of the Anheuser-Busch brewery, had been Lockheed's private residence before he reimagined it as a haven for local artists. Eventually it grew into a bar and restaurant, famous for its jerk chicken and Long Island iced tea in equal measure. Live music has also become an integral part of the Venice experience. Local musicians hit the stage nightly, and the Monday open mic night provides a platform for those with a hankering to get up and express themselves in public.

Drinks and tunes aside, the Venice Cafe is probably best known for its over-the-top visual vibe. The space is a folk art museum of sorts, and every surface, nook, and cranny plays host to myriad eclectic art projects, most of which are the products of Lockheed's fertile imagination. A bar built from the rescued remains of an old boat, found-object mosaics and collages, mannequins adorned with buttons and baubles, and a variety of animal skulls are just some of the eye-catching items on display.

The Venice Cafe is hip but definitely not hipster, more than a bit antiestablishment but with a healthy sense of humor. Cash is king here, no

cards allowed, and don't even think about starting a tab. Check out its famously snarky Facebook page (facebook.com/VeniceCafeStl) to keep up to date on what's going down in the café's colorful confines.

PLATYPUS

4501 Manchester Ave. | 314.359.0824 | drinkplatypus.com

Courtesy of Platypus

Platypus opened in 2021 in the Grove neighborhood, the result of a partnership between Tony Saputo, a longtime fixture on the St. Louis bar scene as a bartender and bar manager, and Meredith Barry, a renowned mixologist who made her bones in Chicago before relocating to the Lou. The idea was to have an ultra-casual neighborhood bar that had top-notch cocktails and could also serve as a live music venue.

Saputo said they took inspiration from some iconic bars when developing the Platypus plan, including installing a Jägermeister frozen drink machine filled with a blend of multiple amari à la Sportsman's Club in Chicago. The small cocktail menu constantly rotates, which means the staff gets to exercise their creativity and aren't beholden to any particular brand or product. Conversely, this careful curation also allows brands the chance to do limited menu takeovers. In the best bar tradition, the cutting-edge cocktail offerings are balanced with plenty of bottled and canned beers. For those who want to get fancy, Busch is available on draft, served up in frozen mugs.

Since Saputo is also a musician (the bar's name is a reference to a Mr. Bungle song), live music was always part of the plan, and it's expanded to three to four nights a week. Platypus has become a home base for up-and-coming touring bands of every genre, from death metal to indie rock and from acoustic folk to hip-hop. Saputo considers it payback for all the spots that supported him and his fellow musicians during his touring days.

Much like its namesake, Platypus is the sum of a multitude of random parts that somehow just work together.

Courtesy of Platypus

NEW SOCIETY

3194 S Grand Blvd. | newsocietystl.com

New Society opened in 2023 in the basement of Monstera Mezcaleria (formerly Grand Spirits Bottle Co.). The concept is a collaboration between chef and mixologist Michael Fricker and mixologist Meredith Barry, and it brings a sense of experimentation and much-needed whimsy to the St. Louis bar scene. The name of the bar is a nod to socialite Clara Bell Walsh, who reportedly held the first cocktail party in St. Louis in 1917. Newspaper reports at the time suggested she was helping to foster a "new society."

While the hidden entrance and cozy confines at New Society might conjure up visions of a speakeasy, it also turns that much-abused Prohibition-era trope on its ear. There's no schtick here. No passwords or restricted access to a select few, and nary a handlebar mustache in sight. But like the original speakeasies, New Society embodies the idea of a place for people to congregate away from the eyes of society at large, especially for members of marginalized groups. Barry said the idea was to create a culinary cocktail experience that was intimate while at the same time being inclusive and fostering connection. All are welcome here.

Pure artistic expression abounds in this tiny 26-seat space. The staff have the freedom to geek out and create cocktails that blur the line between food and drink. Disparate ingredients and flavors usually relegated to the kitchen like tomato water, mozzarella, bread, and even shrimp are combined with the finest spirits, resulting in pure flavor. Themes abound on the menu as well, from tiki-inspired creations to collabs with local artists, providing additional inspiration.

Courtesy of Jason Hackett

New Society is an opportunity to get out of your zone, try something different, and maybe even turn your head toward a new way of thinking.

THE WHISKEY RING

2651 Cherokee St. | 314.669.5817 | facebook.com/thewhiskeyring

Named after a famous conspiracy in the 1870s by a cabal of businessmen and politicians to evade booze taxes, among other nefarious deeds, the Whiskey Ring has gradually become one of the anchors of Cherokee Street. Industry vet John Joern opened the bar in December 2013, when Cherokee Street was in the process of revitalization. New businesses were blossoming, and attractive rents were a thing. According to Joern, he wanted to open a shot-and-a-beer place that was also a hub for community building.

Courtesy of The Whiskey Ring

"I love using the term 'public house.' That's what we are," Joern said. "We get labeled as a dive bar quite often because we don't have sports on TV, and we're not exactly elevated. We're sort of in between those things."

While there are approximately 100 different whiskies on the back bar at any one time, the Whiskey Ring isn't just a whiskey bar. There are plenty of other spirits to be had here, and some really solid cocktails—they make as fine a Manhattan as you'll get anywhere in town. The Ring doesn't have a kitchen, but patrons are more than welcome to bring in their own food, easily done with so many fantastic restaurants in the surrounding blocks.

As befits a neighborhood joint, the Whiskey Ring exhibits a decided lack of pretense when it comes to the decor. Along with bric-a-brac like the enormous steer horns and the vintage Pee Wee Herman doll that preside over the back bar, the Whiskey Ring boasts the best collection of black velvet paintings in town. I'm especially fond of the portrait of Sylvester Stallone as the title character in *Cobra*, arguably his finest role.

THE ROYALE

3132 S Kingshighway Blvd. | 314.772.3600 | theroyale.com

The building at 3132 South Kingshighway Boulevard has been a bar of some sort ever since it was built in 1922, even serving as a speakeasy during the dark days of Prohibition. In 2005 Steven Fitzpatrick Smith bought the place and continued the tradition by reimagining it as the Royale.

Smith had worked in the bar and restaurant business since he was a kid, washing dishes, serving, bartending, and working the door, but his original thought was for his new project to be a music venue. Thankfully he opted for the relative stability of the bar business instead.

First came the bar. The bar program at the Royale was one of the first in town to offer true classic cocktails and the latest craft brews. If memory serves, it was the first local spot I ever heard of that served a Martinez. At some point, food issued forth from the tiny, apartment-sized kitchen. Over the years Smith added an expansive garden and one of the most inviting patios in town. He also created a community, with events like the annual Derby Day soiree, regular record spins from all types of DJs, and political debate watch parties. The Royale hearkens back to the public-house tradition, where the tavern serves as a community center in addition to pouring drinks, and a glance around the space on any given day will reveal a cross section of the neighborhood. Happy-hour drinkers, night owls, hipsters, professors, and tradesmen all feel equally comfortable bellying up to the Royale's bar. It's become more than just a place to grab a drink for a lot of people.

Courtesy of The Royale

Courtesy of The Royale

The Royale celebrated 20 years in April 2025, and it remains Smith's main focus. He has no desire to replicate the Royale elsewhere, which is just as well since intentionally catching that kind of spark would be nearly impossible.

THE VILLAGE BAR

12247 Manchester Rd. | Des Peres | 314.821.4532
facebook.com/VillageBarSTL

The Village Bar in Des Peres holds a special place in my heart. During my college years I worked on a maintenance crew, and my supervisor moonlighted behind the bar there. We'd meet up after work to take advantage of his employee discount, plowing through frosty pitchers of Bud and baskets of fries while we made grand plans for the rest of the evening that never seemed to quite work out. More often than not we'd end up back at the Village, comparing notes and licking our wounds.

Established in 1948, the Village Bar and Grill was originally a feed store before morphing into a drinking and dining destination. In the 1980s the late Joe Pollack wrote a glowing review of the Village's burgers for the *Post-Dispatch*, helping to cement its culinary reputation. The Village is still probably best known for those burgers, though there are plenty of solid bar staples to choose from on the menu. I've always been partial to the hand-cut onion rings myself.

The space has changed more than a bit over the years. The Village expanded into the former wig shop next door a while back, so there's a lot more seating than there was in my so-called heyday. The added square footage has transformed the feel of the place from quasi-dive bar into more of a family-friendly destination. On my last visit, kids in soccer uniforms and their harried parents outnumbered the wizened barflies, which is probably a good thing. The Village still stands out amid the commercial bustle of Manchester Road and remains a go-to for those who want solid eats and cold beer with no pretense.

MUST BE 21
EXIT
Budweiser
BUD & BURGERS
SRIXON
ASK US ABOUT O'FALLON BEERS! O'Fallon

LITTLE LAGER

5848 Hampton Ave. | 314.760.9481 | littlelager.com

Courtesy of Little Lager

In the craft beer world, ales have reigned supreme for years, but lagers have slowly been gaining ground. Here in St. Louis, Little Lager is at the forefront of this shift. The bar specializes in serving up cold-fermented styles like helles, pilsner, Baltic porter, and others that are deemed "lager adjacent," like Kolsch and cold IPA.

Too many bars get wound up about the right way to make a Sazerac or ensuring that wine is served at the correct temperature and in the proper glass, but they neglect how they treat their beers. At Little Lager, draft beers are served up at optimum temperatures via Czech side-pull taps, which create the requisite thick, dense, and creamy foam. The result: pretty much the perfect pint.

The bar is small, with only 22 seats. Likewise, the beers are petite, at least in terms of alcohol by volume. Little Lager is about enjoying quality beers with like-minded individuals, not getting hammered, so sessionable brews are the norm. While beer is taken seriously here, the vibe is anything but uptight.

"I really like dive bars because of the beer-and-shot option, and Little Lager is sort of an elevated take on that," according to owner Manny Negron, though at Little Lager the shots are usually amaro instead of whiskey. The beers available rotate daily, with six to eight selections on tap and up to 30 packaged beers available. There are also nonalcoholic options, ciders, and upward of 40 different amaro for those aforementioned shots. Though Little Lager doesn't have a kitchen, patrons are welcome to bring in their own eats or have them delivered.

Courtesy of Little Lager

ROBUST WINE BAR

227 W Lockwood Ave. | Webster Groves | 314.963.0033 | robustwinebar.com

Courtesy of Arlene Maminta Brown

In recent years Webster Groves has become a culinary destination of sorts for those in the know, with its own very active food and drink scene. One of the cornerstones of said scene is Robust Wine Bar.

Arlene Maminta Browne and her husband, Stanley Browne, opened Robust in 2007, well before Webster was on the foodie map. Back then, there were plenty of restaurants with good wine lists, but wine bars weren't really a thing. Robust was one of the only places really focusec on wine, making it accessible withou pretension and allowing customers to tr different things.

With Arlene's background in marketing and PR and Stanley's wine cred—he's a certified sommelier through the Court o Master Sommeliers and a former wine rep and he comes from a family of oneophiles—Robust quickly became a force in the loca wine community, a position it still holds. Robust gives guests multiple ways tc experience wine, from flights to half pours, and from glass pours to bottles.

The key to the wine menu is the Robust factor. It's a system the Brownes designed that helps guests find the perfect pour based on the body style of the wine. It's also really helpful for those who want to expand their palate and try something new. While the food menu at Robust is designed to work well with wines, it stands on its own, even for those who aren't imbibing. Small-plate and shareable choices abound; I usually gravitate toward the array of cheese plates available.

After all these years, Robust continues to evolve. The bar recently started hosting holiday pop-ups and now has an all-day (noon to 5 p.m.) happy hour with its own menu, called Saturday Social, perfect for those looking to do a little day drinking (and eating).

Courtesy of Arlene Maminta Browne

JOHN D. MCGURK'S IRISH PUB

1200 Russell Blvd. | 314.776.8309 | mcgurks.com

Courtesy of Teri Well

Soulard is one of the most historic enclaves in St. Louis. It also has more bars per capita than probably any other neighborhood in town. To stand out in this crowded field, a place has to be something special, and John D. McGurk's Irish Pub qualifies.

McGurk's opened in 1978 and quickly became the place in St. Louis to hear authentic Celtic music from local musicians and traveling troubadors alike, as well as to get a proper pint. It's been lauded as authentic by authorities as diverse as *Esquire* and *National Geographic*. Over the years, McGurk's has expanded from a corner pub to a fairly sprawling space, but the vibe remains warm and inviting, a public house in the truest sense. Unlike what I call prefab pubs—the ones that spring up in strip walls and are decorated with shamrocks and Jameson banners—there's no kitsch here. Short of traveling to the Emerald Isle you won't find a more authentic Irish pub. Period.

I had popped into McGurk's periodically over the years to grab a drink and listen to some tunes, but I had no real idea about its patio area until I was working on an outdoor drinking and dining story for a local publication and was told I had to check it out. To call this space a patio is sort of a disservice. This 15,000-square-foot outdoor area features three separate bars, tons of seating, plenty of beautiful water features, and abundant greenery.

I highly recommend going to McGurk's of an evening, ordering a plate of bangers and mash or maybe some Guinness stew, indulging in a pint or maybe a nip of something stronger, and enjoying some music and community.

SASHA'S WINE BAR/ SASHA'S ON SHAW

Sasha's Wine Bar | 706 DeMun Ave. | Clayton | 314.863.7274
Sasha's on Shaw | 4069 Shaw Ave. | 314.771.7274 | sashaswinebar.com

Courtesy of Sasha's

St. Louis has always been a beer town, but there's a sizable community of oenophiles here as well. For a long time this group of imbibers had limited options. But that was before visionary Alan Richman opened Sasha's Wine Bar on DeMun Avenue in Clayton and Sasha's on Shaw in the Shaw neighborhood. These two have been serving fans of the grape for decades (22 and 17 years, respectively) and are cornerstones of the local wine world.

Both of these stalwarts of the St. Louis beverage scene opened up before wine bars were much of a thing in town, and they became beacons in their respective neighborhoods, developing unique personalities all their own that reflect the enclaves they're a part of. Both spots are open seven days a week with almost identical food menus, focusing on Mediterranean-style small plates as well as a few larger entrée options. While the Sasha's wine lists are similar in concept, specific labels on hand differ somewhat. Shaw tends to focus on what's new and adventurous in its offerings, while DeMun skews a bit more conservative.

What I've always admired about both Sasha's is the lack of pretense and the breadth of the wines available. There are 52 by-the-glass wines at DeMun and 55 at Shaw, with many half pours available. Even if wine isn't your thing, there are plenty of spirits, cocktails, and beers available along with low-alcohol-by-volume and nonalcoholic options.

Even though I'm very much a wine rookie I've always felt comfortable at both of these legacy bars. I've always especially enjoyed the cozy hearth area at Shaw. There's nothing like sipping your favorite libation in front of a roaring fire and letting the world pass you by.

FOX & HOUNDS TAVERN

6300 Clayton Rd. | Clayton | 314.647.7300 | cheshirestl.com

I've always been fascinated by the Cheshire Inn. Sitting at the off-kilter confluence of Clayton Road, I 64/40, and Skinker Boulevard/McCausland Avenue in all of its faux-Tudor glory, it always seemed more like part of a bucolic English village or an upscale Ren faire site than a hotel to me. I've never gotten around to staycationing there, but I've always been fond of its in-house tavern, Fox & Hounds, one of the more unique watering holes in town.

This pub gets my absolute highest rating for overall coziness, thanks in large part to the rustic stone hearth and fireplace at the center of it all. The decor is meant to simulate an English manor house, or at least the American idea of one. Taxidermied critters, exposed wooden beams, and plush seating abound. Having never spent any time in the English countryside, I can't vouch for the authenticity of the space. However, it's supremely comfy, inviting, and unquestionably unique. It's easy to while away an evening in front of the fire, sipping whiskey and thinking large thoughts.

Aesthetics aside, Fox & Hounds has a really good selection of spirits, including

whiskies from both sides of the pond. The bar has everything to whip up almost any classic cocktail that comes to mind, and there's a rotating menu of original drinks too. There's a fairly substantial food menu as well for those who need a bite between rounds. I usually go for the fish and chips or the shepard's pie when I visit for the full UK experience. True anglophiles can even get a yard of ale to slake their thirst, though advise having your Uber app at the ready if you go down that road. This is not the usual hotel bar by a long shot.

SPORTSMAN'S PARK

9901 Clayton Rd. | Ladue | 314.991.3381 | sportsmansparkladue.com

I'm not what you'd call sporty, so those who know me may be surprised that I'm including Sportsman's Park here. After all, it's named after a famous ballyard from long ago, and it's chock-full of memorabilia from pretty much every St. Louis sports team that ever played. I mean, they even have bar tables shaped like footballs. But I would argue that Sportsman's is not merely a "sports bar" but actually exists in the more rarified realm of "neighborhood bar."

Sportsman's originally opened as Jackie's Place in 1974, a nod to co-owner Jackie Smith of the late football Cardinals. Smith opted out after a while, and the place was renamed Sportsman's Park. While sports is the overarching theme of the place, Sportsman's (thankfully) doesn't have the ridiculous scale common in what's usually regarded as a sports bar. There are TVs broadcasting the day's game, but they're of reasonable size. The memorabilia isn't behind glass, but right out in the open, and there's not an energy drink poster in sight. Clearly someone has lovingly collected all of those autographs, jerseys, and hats. It all feels more about local history than any particular team or game. In fact, during my visits I've never seen anyone screaming at the screen, arguing calls with the ref, or

berating a bumbling player. Instead, there's usually a group of duffers at the bar solving the world's problems. Someone's telling the bartender about their day. A couple of old friends are sitting at a corner two-top catching up. Whatever game is on is a part of the atmosphere but not the main event.

The menu is full of cheesy puns (Ty Cobb salad? Heyyooooooo!), which just adds to the charm. The beer is cold, the burgers are tasty, and tater tots are an optional side, something I think the world needs more of.

THE GIN ROOM

3200 S Grand Blvd | 314.771.3411 | natashasginroom.com

Natasha Bahrami developed her love of gin in her early 20s when a bartender at a now-forgotten spot in the Central West End served up her first dirty gin martini. This paved the way to what would eventually become the Gin Room.

Bahrami grew up in the restaurant industry. Her folks emigrated from Iran and opened Little Kitchen in 1983 in downtown St. Louis. They eventually renamed the restaurant Cafe Natasha in honor of their daughter and relocated to South Grand in 2001. Though Bahrami would leave St. Louis to pursue another career, the pull of her hometown and the restaurant drew her back. In 2014 she turned the bar at Cafe Natasha into the Gin Room, with the mission of spreading the word about her favorite spirit.

To say Bahrami's baby has been successful is the grossest of understatements. In the ensuing years the Gin Room has received accolades almost too numerous to mention. Some of the highlights include a James Beard Award nomination for Outstanding Bar in 2023 and a place on the *Imbibe* magazine 75 list in 2025. Bahrami herself got a Beard nomination in 2025 for Outstanding Professional in Beverage Service, and she was inducted into *Gin* magazine's Gin Hall of Fame in 2021.

These days, the back bar at the Gin Room boasts more than 400 gins and a rotating cocktail list that features the spirit (and others) in a multitude of creative ways. The Gin Room also offers gin flights so guests can try various iterations side by side and a plethora of tonics to mix with. The Gin Room has also become known for its educational focus, holding distiller seminars, classes, and tastings on the regular. In 2015 Bahrami founded Gin Week, a festival celebrating all things gin. The event eventually went national, was renamed Gin World, and now encompasses 15 cities across the country, including St. Louis.

Courtesy of Natasha Bahrami

THE SCOTTISH ARMS

6 S Sarah St. | thescottisharms.com

There are many bars and restaurants around town that hold special places in my wizened, dried-up heart, but maybe none more so than the Scottish Arms. Since it first opened in 2005, this UK-style public house was a place where I felt as comfortable as I would in front of my own hearth.

The hearty menu at the Arms never failed to satisfy. It was the only place where a Midwesterner could get a plate of authentic haggis (minus the sheep stomach, which is verboten on these shores). The Arms also had the best fish and chips; if it had come wrapped in newspaper I wouldn't have been able to differentiate the dish from the best examples from across the pond. I've always preferred Scotch over other whiskies, and back in my drinking days I looked at the back bar at the Arms as my personal single-malt playground. A wee dram and a pint beside and I'd be set. Even more comforting than the food and drink was the hospitality and community. During almost every visit I'd run into someone I knew. We'd often retire to the glorious back patio for another round or two.

It's a sad fact that bars and restaurants come and go. It's a tough business, and I have to admit that more often than not I'm not particularly affected by news of closures. But when it was announced in July of 2024 that the Arms was shuttering, it hit me in the gut. Hard. The farewell service was full of stories and tears, and when the pipers played at the end of the night it seemed so very final. Thankfully, another ownership group was able to step in and save the Arms and preserve its legacy, and I no longer have to refer to the old gal in the past tense. Slainte.

Scottish Arms
THE
SCOTTISH
ARMS
PUBLIC HOUSE
8

RESTAURANTS

HENDEL'S

599 Rue St. Denis St. | Florissant | 314.837.2304
hendelsrestaurant.com

Courtesy of Hendel's Restaurant

Even in a historical enclave like Old Town Florissant, Hendel's stands out. The building itself dates from 1873 and originally served the area as a general store. It was purchased by the Hendel family in 1915 and for the next 78 years was a combination grocery store and butcher shop. In 1994, the building was purchased by Ed Bennett, a Florissant restaurateur and history aficionado who fell in love with the old edifice. He in turn converted the space into a restaurant and named it after the former owners. When Ed passed away in 2008, his son Nate and Nate's wife, Christina, took over Hendel's, and the duo has worked tirelessly since then to keep the eatery a vital part of the neighborhood.

Over the years the space has changed some. The front porch was expanded in 2003, and in 2009 the bar area was

Courtesy of Jessica Harmon

added using bricks and flooring rescued from an old church. These additions have kept Hendel's current and competitive while still respecting the building's status as a historical landmark. While the vibe at Hendel's is more casual these days—the white tablecloths and server uniforms were abandoned in the mid-2000s—it remains a place where people get together to celebrate life's big moments or just the end of the work week.

According to Nate, Hendel's food menu is tweaked periodically but there are plenty of dishes that won't be going anywhere, like the fan favorite Cajun carbonara, a combo of shrimp, andouille sausage, tomatoes, scallions, and a Cajun cream sauce served over linguine, which has been available since Day 1.

Thirty years is a heck of a run for a restaurant these days, but according to Nate, the key to Hendel's longevity isn't a secret—just a combination of commitment and community.

"[Christina and I] both really care about the place," he said. "And Florissant has always been there for us."

ROCK STAR TACOS

4916 Shaw Ave. | 314.571.9016 | rockstartacos.com

The inspiration for Rock Star Tacos came after a gig when co-owner and executive chef Wil Pelly and a bandmate came up with the idea for a rock-themed taco shack. Pelly, who plays bass in various local bands, and his business/life partner, Rebecca Schaaf, who teaches voice and piano, thought merging their love of music and food was a no-brainer, and they proceeded to open the first version of Rock Star in 2019 in a tiny walk-up kiosk in the New Town development in St. Charles. In 2022 they moved to more spacious digs in the Gaslight building in the Hill neighborhood.

Rock Star is nothing if not funky and fun. Most surfaces are covered with an ever-growing collection of musical memorabilia, and the menu is full of pun-laden names referencing musicians and song titles. Some of the most popular tacos on the menu include the Shrimp Bizkit (pan-seared shrimp with peppers and onions), Fish You Were Here (deep-fried cod) and the Notorious P.I.G. (crispy chipotle honey pork belly with cilantro and onions). Sides get the Rock Star treatment as well, like the Fry of the Tiger french fries and Mac 'n Diane mac and cheese. Customers can nosh on these and many other delights while admiring the scattered musical memorabilia throughout the dining room and bar.

Rock Star also offers catering and has developed a following as the place tour managers hit up when they need quality eats to feed their bands and crews who're passing through the Lou. Musical luminaries Billy Gibbons of ZZ Top and Alice Cooper are among the rockers who are die-hard fans and repeat customers.

NUDO HOUSE

multiple locations | 314.274.8046 | nudohousestl.com

Qui Tran loves soup, which is evident in the tasty panopoly of broths, soups, and stocks served up at his other restaurant, Mai Lee. While Vietnamese soups like phos and hot pots take center stage at Mai Lee, Tran decided to focus on Japanese ramen for his second venture, Nudo House. The first Nudo House opened in 2017 in Creve Coeur, and inside of a year it was featured on the cover of *Food & Wine* (though the photo printed was of beef pho, not ramen). The restaurant proved so successful that a second location opened in late 2019 just inside the St. Louis city limits.

Ramen-heads are notoriously picky, so Tran knew he had to get it right before he brought the concept to the public. Not one to do things halfway, Tran and business partner/chief collaborator Chef Marie-Anne Velasco went big, touring the US in search of the best bowls of ramen, all in the name of research. Eventually they met and trained under Chef Shigetoshi Nakamura, one of Japan's four "Ramen Gods," in order to learn the fine points of the art of this classic Japanese noodle soup before introducing their vision to the public via a series of pop-ups.

Courtesy of Nudo House

That Tran and Velasco respect the cuisine is evident in the carefully curated ramen selection, which ranges from the Classic Nudo (tonkotsu broth, shoyu, chasu pork, menna, and black garlic) to the Hebrew Hammer, a playful take on Jewish chicken soup featuring chicken thigh and a luxurious broth. The menu also has a section dubbed Not Ramen with favorites like crab rangoon and spring rolls, plus there are phos, bahn mi sandwiches, and a plethora of other dishes that reflect the flavors of Vietnam, China, Japan, and the Philippines. Guests can slurp to their hearts' content in the colorful and roomy dining room decorated with accents of anime images (especially Tran's favorite, St. Louis's own Voltron) and traditional Japanese art. Like the restaurant's name, which is a child's take on the word *noodle*, the Nudo space is bright, playful, and anything but serious.

Courtesy of Nudo House

FAILONI'S

6715 Manchester Ave. | 314.781.5221 | failonisrestaurantbar.com

It really doesn't get more old-school than Failoni's. The humble brick building in the Franz Park neighborhood has been home to this popular bar and restaurant since 1916, when founder Alessandro Failoni bought the site from Lemp Brewery with the plan to serve the workers at Scullen Steel, then located across the street. The restaurant has been through its share of iterations, including serving as a speakeasy during Prohibition, but through it all Failoni's has been a family affair, with four generations having worked or currently working in the front and the back of the house to secure its legacy. As third-generation owner Vic Failoni said, "It's not just a bar. We look at it as our house."

While bellying up to the bar at Failoni's for a frosty cold one or a nip of something a bit harder is a neighborhood tradition, there's also a full food menu of scratch-made favorites. The menu ranges from sandwiches to salads to pastas, but the eatery is probably best known for its brick-oven pizzas. Want to savor a Failoni's pizza in the comfort of your own home? Half-baked pies are available to go.

Courtesy of Failoni's

Since the 1980s, live music has been a staple at Failoni's. First there was an accordion player; then Vic's brother, the late Alex Failoni Jr., began crooning Sinatra and other favorites and drawing in a whole new crowd, establishing a tuneful tradition that continues to thrive. I used to have a boss who was a die-hard Sinatra fan and he swore that if he listened to Frank and Alex with his eyes closed he couldn't tell the difference.

While the space itself has expanded over the years and the neighborhood has evolved, one thing has remained constant—Failoni's commitment to family, food, and friends.

BALKAN TREAT BOX

8103 Big Bend Blvd. | 314.733.5700 | balkantreatbox.com

Back in 2016, a bright red and blue truck debuted in St. Louis's then-burgeoning food truck scene, helmed by the husband and wife team of Loryn and Edo Nalic. Dubbed Balkan Treat Box, the truck's menu featured flavors from countries in the Balkan Peninsula, including Edo's native Bosnia, along with Croatia, Albania, Turkey, and Serbia. The truck quickly became one of the top mobile eateries in town, and that success led to the Nalics opening a permanent home for Balkan Treat Box in Webster Groves in 2019.

The heart of the operation is a large wood oven, used to create baked delicacies like somun, a soft, pillowy flatbread that serves as the foundation for many of Balkan's creations. Despite the delicious depth of the menu, I almost always fall back on the cevapi, a hearty sandwich made with grilled sausage tucked inside a warm somun. I've also been known to take down a pide on occasion—Turkish flatbread topped with a choice of meats (beef is my personal fave); kajmak, a tangy fresh cheese; and ajvar, a sweet and earthy condiment made from bell peppers and eggplant.

All of this goodness has resulted in numerous awards and accolades for the Balkan team from local publications and the national press as well, including Eater, *Bon Appétit*, *Food & Wine*, and *Esquire*. Loryn has also been honored four times as a nominee for the James Beard Awards Best Chef: Midwest.

Courtesy of Spencer Pernikoff

These days there are a couple of additional spots to enjoy the fruits of the Nalics' labors. Balkan now has a concession at Energizer Park, home of St. Louis City SC, and the duo recently opened up another concept, Telva at the Ridge, inside Rolling Ridge Nursery in Webster Groves.

WONTON KING

8116 Olive Blvd. | University City | 314.567.9997 | asianfoodstl.com

The stretch of Olive Boulevard from roughly I-170 to Skinker, cutting through Olivette and University City, is a treasure trove of international flavors. These blocks contain myriad stores and restaurants offering up the cuisines of dozens of cultures, and we St. Louisans are lucky to have this bounty in our backyard just waiting to be sampled.

One of my favorite places to grab a bite on Olive is Wonton King. This humble Chinese restaurant puts out fantastic food with little pretense. There are no opulent color palates or exotic knicknacks to be had here, just an enticing array of dishes, from crowd-pleasers like crab rangoon, sweet and sour pork, and seemingly endless variations of fried rice and noodle dishes, to more esoteric fare—at least in Middle America—like congees (rice porridge).

While the lunch and dinner menus are certainly full of delicious offerings, for me Wonton King comes into its own with its dim sum service, where carts full of smallish bites make their way from table to table in plates, bowls, and steamers filled with all manner of goodness. Think brunch but infinitely more diverse, and as a result, tastier. Wonton King puts out classics like siu mai, steamed dumplings usually filled with pork or prawn, and steamed buns filled with weet-and-savory roasted pork known as char siu. While these favorites seem to attract the most

attention from diners, there are dozens of other delights to be had inside those steamers, from chicken feet to bok choy. My advice is to gather a group of friends, tuck into one of the large tables with a lazy susan in the center, and say yes to every dish that comes by.

NEON GREENS

4176 Manchester Ave. | 314.899.0400 | neongreens.com

Like so many folks during COVID, Josh Smith, owner and founder of Neon Greens, found himself out of sorts. He left New York City, where he'd worked for 11 years as a set designer for film and television, and went upstate to live in a small cottage and ride out the pandemic. To keep himself occupied, Smith started growing food hydroponically, a technique that eschews soil and utilizes water instead, making it possible to grow plants almost anywhere.

"I started growing anything and everything I could get my hands on," Smith said, and the produce he was producing was better than anything he'd ever found in a store. He realized people would eat more vegetables if they all tasted as good as what he was growing, and he decided to scale up. Smith's original plan was to develop and sell modular hydroponic units. That idea morphed into a marriage of a hypdroponic farm and a restaurant, the perfect way to connect people with their food and perhaps inspire them to grow their own. As Smith said, "We can all make salads together."

The idea snowballed, and in just under two years Smith returned to his native St. Louis and opened Neon Greens in the Grove. The farm itself came first, growing as much produce as three acres of land in a 40-by-8-foot space. Smith began selling produce to local restaurants, funding the restaurant side of the operation, which debuted in the spring of 2024. The menu features a seasonally rotating array of salads that showcase the best and freshest vegetables in town.

Free tours of Neon Greens's hydroponic farm are offered Mondays, Wednesdays, and Fridays at 1 p.m., and more in-depth classes and tours are available monthly.

Courtesy of Neon Greens

THE FOUNDRY FOOD HALL

3730 Foundry Way | cityfoundrystl.com

Courtesy of The Foundry

The concept of food halls makes a lot of sense—a space where multiple culinary concepts exist side by side, offering the curious diner myriad choices of cuisine and local restaurateurs a place to showcase what they can do to an ever-evolving clientele. While these types of developments are de rigueur in larger markets like New York City and Chicago, St. Louis didn't really have one until the Foundry Food Hall opened in Midtown in 2023.

The Foundry Food Hall is part of a larger development called City Foundry STL, which also houses entertainment venues like Alamo Drafthouse for movies

Courtesy of The Foundry

and City Winery for live music as well as plenty of retail shops. I like to think of the development as a one-stop date night. The 15-acre property was owned by City Electric at one time and was a hub of manufacturing before ceasing production. It languished for years before being reimagined in its current form by the Lawrence Group.

As the name implies, the Foundry Food Hall is basically a large open space broken up into stalls where individual proprietors do their thing and various community tables are scattered about for diners to devour their finds. There are 17 restaurants represented on the main level, from pizza to poke, burgers to barbecue, and then some. It's the perfect scenario for the individual foodie to sample a variety of cuisines, but it's also ideal for large groups that can't settle on one particular place to eat.

The Foundry website gives a good rundown of each of the restaurants represented and the gluten-free, vegan, and vegetarian options available across all of the concepts. Gift cards good at any establishment in the hall are also available.

ROPER'S RIBS

6929 W Florissant Ave. | Jennings | 314.381.6200 | ropersribs.com

Roper's Ribs, located at the corner of Jennings Station Road and West Florissant Ave., is a legendary spot for St. Louis barbecue. Carl and Denise Roper have been serving up classic 'cue at this location for 32 years, slowly perfecting their menu and becoming one of those places where those who know what's up go for true meaty bliss.

Usually Carl is behind the scenes manning the kitchen and Denise is working the counter talking up the customers, and she's a font of good advice on what to order. Of course, trying the ribs here is mandatory, but there are plenty of other delicacies available on the menu. Rib tips, pulled pork, and beef burnt ends are all stellar choices. One benchmark I use for traditional barbecue is snoots. This off-cut is hard to do well—undercooked and they're flabby, overdone and it's like cracking into cardboard. Roper's snoots, though, have just the right amount of give when you bite into them. The last time I stopped in, Denise schooled me on the proper way to order snoots as well—FYI, the key is getting the sauce on the side if you're ordering to go to keep them from getting soft.

The postage stamp–size dining room at Roper's is decorated with autographs from all of the celebrity fans who have stopped in or otherwise enjoyed Roper's food over the years, like Steve Harvey, along with the various awards the Ropers have accumulated. The two-tops dressed up in classic red-and-white-checked tablecloths solidify the classic feel of the place. On busy days the tiny space fills up fast, but it's more than worth the wait. They also sell their dry rub blend for those who want to try their hand at replicating that Roper's magic at home.

BARTOLINO'S OSTERIA

2103 Sulphur Ave. | 314.644.2266 | bartolinosrestaurants.com

Bartolino's Osteria is one of those places that doesn't get mentioned much when favorite Italian places on the Hill are mentioned. The restaurant used to be located just up the street on Hampton Avenue on the edge of that venerable neighborhood. In 2008 Bartolino's moved to its current location adjacent to the Drury Inn & Suites at Forest Park (and added Osteria to its name).

The elegantly casual dining room, recently redesigned by Space Architects, Designers + Builders, has plenty of elbow room, and there's also a spacious separate bar area as well as seasonal outdoor seating, so you can pick your own vibe. While atmosphere is important, the food should be the main event at any restaurant, and Bartolino's has an expansive menu full of all the heavy hitters of Italian cuisine. All manner of pastas and risottos can be had here along with plenty of prime cuts and seafood. It goes without saying that local fave toasted ravioli makes an appearance on the menu, as does St. Louis–style pizza. Now, I'm a staunch and unwavering fan of the traditional St. Louis pie. Don't even attempt to engage me in the thin crust versus thick crust, provel versus mozzarella debate. I've always steered clear of naming my favorite version of our beloved thin crust delicacy. However, I'm willing to go

on record as saying that Bartolino's has two of my favorite versions: the Bartolino's Special with sausage, onion, mushrooms, and pepperoni, and the Veggie, topped with artichoke hearts, tomato, mushrooms, onions, and peppers.

To those who hail from outside the city and balk at crossing over the county line, Bartolino's Osteria is right off I-44, and there's plenty of parking. No excuses.

HOUSE OF INDIA

8501 Delmar Blvd. | University City | 314.567.6850 | hoistl.com

I became a fan of House of India years ago when my wife turned me on to their daily lunch buffet, a really tasty and affordable deal. Unfortunately, the buffet didn't survive COVID intact; these days it's only available on Sundays. But though that inexpensive lunch spread brought me in, the food itself is what keeps me coming back.

Since 1995, House of India has been a local bastion of Indian cuisine in St. Louis. Now, I definitely appreciate culinary creativity and pushing the boundaries of cuisine and what not. But I also highly value tradition and consistency, and House of India has both of those elements in abundance. The food is traditional and blessedly free of fusion, riffs, and mash-ups. What you get instead are classic Indian dishes made with utmost care and zero pretense. The menu is fairly expansive, with pretty much all of the Indian favorites represented, including lamb, chicken, and seafood dishes, veggie options, tandoori, and several versions of soft nan bread. It might be a rookie move, but I rarely stray from a few faves when I order. I usually tuck into some chicken tikka masala or a paneer dish and wash it down with a mango lassi. Someday I'll roam to another part of the menu and explore a bit more, but it's hard to stray from the tried and true when it's this good.

I find the dining rooms at House of India as comfortable as the food. Some of

the pictures hanging on the walls are slightly askew, the carpet is reminiscent of a hotel hallway, and sheets of white butcher paper are laid across the tables for easy cleanup. The place feels lived in and welcoming. These days House of India also does a brisk carryout business, as evidenced by the multiple bags of orders waiting for pickup at the host stand whenever I stop by.

MESKEREM

3210 S Grand Blvd. | 314.772.4442 | meskeremstl.com

South Grand Boulevard between I-44 and, say, Chippewa Street, is home to a wide variety of restaurants serving up "ethnic" foods, many of them hard or impossible to come by in other areas of the city and county. One of my personal favorites along this golden route is Meskerem, which specializes in Ethiopian cuisine. Any type of African food is hard to come by in these parts, which makes Meskerem a true gem, and it's been a cornerstone of the South Grand dining scene since opening its doors in 2007.

There are plenty of meaty dishes on the Meskerem menu, featuring lamb, chicken, and beef. Though I definitely fall into the carnivore category, I'm usually drawn to Meskerem's veggie options when I visit. Gomen wat, steamed collard greens with plenty of ginger and garlic, and butecha, a spicy chickpea dish, are just two of my favorites here. I absolutely love it when restaurants offer combo platters of their greatest hits, as it gives diners a chance to get a tasty overview of a menu without committing to any one dish. Meskerem offers a couple of combos, including the Vegetarian Combo for One, which has both the aforementioned gomen wat and butecha in addition to miser alecha and miser wat, both spicy lentil-based dishes, among other bites.

One aspect of the Meskerem dining experience that locals might not get is that no utensils are used. Instead, guests tear off pieces of injera, a spongy, tangy flatbread, and use it to scoop up their bites. The bread adds a unique texture to each morsel and serves as a tasty way to break the ice if you're dining with a group. Do not be the person who asks for a fork. Do not bring your own.

THE MUD HOUSE

2101 Cherokee St. | 314.776.6599 | themudhousestl.com

Coffee shops are a dime a dozen. For me, most of them just serve as coworking spaces, good for free Wi-Fi, a jolt of caffeine, and little more. The Mud House, though, is quite another matter.

I've been frequenting the Mud House for years, ever since I first stumbled across it one morning as I poked around the vintage stores that line the east side of Cherokee Street. It's located in a historic corner building at the intersection of Cherokee Street and Illinois Avenue. Thankfully, ownership never deigned to "modernize" the facade by covering up the original red brick or adding any unnecessary flair to the joint. The interior of the Mud House brings many words to mind. Cozy. Inviting. Ecclectic for sure, thanks to the unpretentious kitsch of the vintage typewriters and taxidermied critter heads that watch over the counter and dining room.

The house java, roasted by Blueprint Coffee, is mighty tasty, and teas from local fave Big Heart Tea Co. are available as well. But the Mud House is known as much for its food as for its beverage options, and a number of talented chefs have come up through its micro kitchen. A menu favorite of mine is the minimally monikered Burrito, a tortilla stuffed to bursting with scrambled eggs, potatoes, cheese, and probably the best black bean chili around.

Once you put your order in, I suggest perusing the used books for sale in the back of the dining room, and then taking advantage of the stellar people-watching opportunities. The last time I dropped in, there was someone sitting out front apparently repairing doorknobs. There's also a surprisingly spacious outdoor seating area around back for those who prefer to enjoy their coffee alfresco when weather permits.

nut dept.
EXIT
it's gonna be

PAPPY'S SMOKEHOUSE

Multiple locations | pappyssmokehouse.com

Founded in 2008, Pappy's Smokehouse is usually the place the conversation about modern barbecue in St. Louis starts and ends. Located in the heart of Midtown, Pappy's has become known far and wide for its meaty wares, garnering numerous awards and slots on myriad best-of lists.

Courtesy of Pappy's Smokehouse

Early on in the Pappy's timeline, the restaurant was visited by Adam Richman for his *Man v. Food* show, which helped thrust the eatery into the national spotlight. It was the first time that I remember a local restaurant making an appearance on a big-time TV show like that, and it was quite the talk of the town's culinary circles at the time. Richman is honored on the Pappy's menu with the "Adam Bomb" combo, a full slab of ribs, three sandwiches—beef brisket, pork, and smoked chicken—plus four sides and a hot link Frito pie.

The name of the restaurant is an homage to founder Mike Emerson's brother Jim, whose nickname was Pappy, and it's a delicious tribute to his memory. Pappy's specializes in pork-heavy Memphis-style barbecue, dry rubbed and slow cooked over cherry and applewood for up to 24 hours. Like many barbecue joints, the ribs are the main attraction at Pappy's, but the menu holds many more flavorful options. I usually opt for the pulled pork sandwich, the aftermath of which requires most of a roll of paper towels to make me presentable enough to go back out in public. The sides are solid as well; the baked beans and vinegar slaw aren't to be missed.

Courtesy of Pappy's Smokehouse

These days there's a second Pappy's in St. Peters to take care of the West County crowd. Whichever location you choose, though, it's important to remember not to drag your heels getting there. Pappy's often sells out early, and when the meat is gone, it's gone.

TASTE OF BOSNIA

3970 N Union Rd. | Mehlville | 314.329.6223 | tasteofbosniastl.com

Sometimes the best things come in the most humble of wrappers. Take Taste of Bosnia. It's in a fairly nondescript building located next to a monolithic megachurch, in the middle of a decidedly uninspiring stretch of Union Road in South St. Louis County. While very little is happening on the outside, inside Taste of Bosnia, owners Elvira and Emil Ahmetspahic are serving up some serious comfort food.

The Ahmetspahics opened the restaurant in 2021. Elvira, who had gone to culinary school in Bosnia, immediately put her training to work. The menu has a slew of Bosnian favorites, like sarme, pickled cabbage leaves stuffed full of rice and ground beef, and cevapi, grilled sausages served in lepinja, a soft Bosnian flatbread. Fresh soups are one of Taste of Bosnia's signature offerings as well. Try a bowl of trahana, a traditional soup with sourdough noodles, veggies, and your choice of beef or chicken, and see if you agree. Not sure just what to order from this list of deliciousness? I suggest first-timers try out the mjesano meso, a meaty sampler platter that includes grilled chicken, cevapi, and pljeskavica, a Bosnian burger patty of sorts, along with fries and plenty of lepinja. Catering is also available.

The cozy dining room seats about 20 and fills up fast, especially on the weekends, but takeout is always available. If you want to be the hit of your next office party or family get-together, catering is also an option. I also suggest striking up a conversation with the owners when you visit. You won't find a friendlier pair anywhere.

LONA'S LIL EATS

2199 California Ave. | 314.925.8938 | lonaslileats.com

Lona Powers's story reads like a Netflix documentary. Born and raised in a small village in rural China, she made her way to St. Louis, her then-husband's hometown. After working for some other places around town, notably Nobu's in University City, Powers decided to strike out on her own. In 2008 she started a food stand at Soulard Farmers Market featuring her signature rice-paper wraps. The booth proved so popular she was eventually able to open her own brick-and-mortar store in Fox Park in 2014 and give Lona's Lil Eats a permanent home.

It's a great tale, full of passion, tenacity, and plenty of tasty bites. Powers's village is located in the southern part of China, home to many ethnic minorities, and she was exposed to the flavors of Burma (now Myanmar), Thailand, Vietnam, and Laos as well as traditional regional Chinese dishes. Powers's food takes cues from all of these influences. The menu at Lona's is nothing if not inclusive, with plenty of choices for vegans, vegetarians, and carnivores alike. As noted previously, the centerpiece of Lona's menu is the massive rice-paper wraps (also available as a plate sans the wrapper or with a flour tortilla). There are a couple of variations available, but I almost always choose the build-your-own option. My favorite wrap version includes cold glass noodles and shrimp, and I'm always sure to get a side of the earthy, spicy bamboo stew.

Powers's nose-to-the-grindstone ethos and dedication to craft has led to a string of awards and recognition, including a James Beard Awards nomination for Best Chef: Midwest in 2018. When Powers was informed of the honor, she first asked what it was, then turned her attention back to the kitchen. Legend.

Courtesy of Phil Kurrus

CROWN CANDY KITCHEN

1401 St. Louis Ave. | 314.621.9650 | crowncandykitchen.net

Crown Candy Kitchen is truly a culinary and cultural landmark in St. Louis. Opened up by friends Harry Karandzieff and Pete Jugaloff in 1913, the confectionary/eatery retains much of that early-20th-century feel. Ducking under the striped awning and entering the building is akin to entering a time machine. The walls are adorned with vintage Coca-Cola memorabilia, and the ceiling fans suspended from the vintage tin ceiling spin lazily. The shop was taken over by Harry's son George in the 1950s and is now run by his three grandsons, Andy, Tommy, and Mike, who have brought this venerable spot into the new millennium while retaining its classic vibe.

The soda fountain serves up confections like phosphates, malteds, and sundaes. Those who think they have what it takes can attempt the Five Malt Challenge—drink five malts (or shakes) in 30 minutes and they're free, plus you get honored on the wall of winners and take home a T-shirt to boot. Crown Candy still makes its own chocolate and offers a variety of assorted candies made with it, along with a plethora of other sweet treats, at the candy counter. For those who need something more than just sweets, the food menu covers all of the comfort food bases. Highlights include house-made chili, available in chili mac, chili dog, chili tamale, and solo forms, and signature sandwiches like the Heart Stopper BLT, a customer favorite served up on white bread toast with plenty of Miracle Whip.

While the quality comestibles keep Crown Candy at the top of the culinary heap, the restaurant is equally important for its dedication to its neighborhood. Years of white flight and general neglect by the powers that be have decimated many areas of North St. Louis, but instead of relocating, Crown Candy remains invested in its roots.

BISTRO LA FLORAISON

7637 Wydown Blvd. | Clayton | 314.725.8880 | bistrolafloraison.com

The intersection of Wydown Boulevard and Hanley Road in Clayton has long been what I consider to be a hot corner for St. Louis restaurants. Some renowned eateries have called, and continue to call, this block home. To be successful here a restaurant needs to be something special, and Bistro La Floraison more than fits the bill.

Take Root Hospitality, which also owns Winslow's Table and Vicia, opened Bistro La Floraison in 2022. The concept of an upscale Parisian eatery may seem outdated in this era of flash and fusion, but this quaint spot stands as a welcome respite from the maelstrom of the local restaurant scene.

Bistro's location used to be two businesses back in the day, a cobbler and a barbershop. Fun fact: I used to frequent both of these establishments on the regular back in the '90s. The neighboring spaces merged and for many years the space was home to another beloved eatery, Bar Les Freres, before COVID had its way. I've never been a big fan of the fussy white tablecloth experience, but Bistro La Floraison manages to be as elegant and elevated as any fine dining place while at the same time being eminently accessible. It's a welcome departure from the glitter and glass of downtown Clayton just a few blocks away.

The food menu here tends toward French favorites as one would expect, sometimes with a twist or two. A prime example is the fried chicken cordon bleu, a crispy take on the classic dish that has been on the menu since Day 1 and was only recently retired. I have worked behind the stick at Bistro, and I can attest that the tiny but mighty four-seat bar puts out solid cocktails, both classic and original, and boasts a wine list filled with some fine Old World vino.

Courtesy of Take Root Hospitality

KAIN TAYO

2700 Locust St. | 314.396.2110 | kaintayotrenton.wordpress.com/food

It's really gratifying to see Filipino food gaining popularity in St. Louis, with places like the late, great Guerrilla Street Food and the Fatted Caf bringing the cuisine to the hungry masses. One of the more recent Filipino restaurants to open its doors in town is Kain Tayo, and it's quickly become a favorite of the Filipino diaspora and others who have an affinity for delicious food.

Randy and Sally Arcega opened Kain Tayo in Trenton, Illinois, in 2019, spurred on by friends and acquaintances who fell in love with Sally's cooking. They moved operations to St. Louis in 2023, setting up shop in Midtown. Kain Tayo means "let's eat" in Tagolog, one of the main languages spoken in the Philippines. It's an apt moniker, because the restaurant serves up a really expansive menu of favorites. Most of the dishes are based on Sally's family recipes and represent some of the foundational flavors of the country. For those who don't know much about Filipino food, I'd say start with Chef Sally's Sisig, which mixes in fried chicken thigh meat with the traditional pork in a spicy proprietary sauce. It's delicious and comforting, and it's a perfect gateway to exploring the panoply of Filipino flavors and dishes.

I was lucky enough to get my first tastes of Filipino food in the Philippines many years ago. More than 7,000 islands make up the country, so claiming I know anything about its food based on a few months in Manilla is ridiculous. However, I did gain a real appreciation for the cuisine and the country as a whole, and eating at Kain Tayo reminds me of why.

Courtesy of Sally Arcega

GIOIA'S DELI

multiple locations | gioiasdeli.com

Bring up the subject of tradition in the St. Louis food scene and Gioia's Deli is bound to be one of the first places mentioned. Gioia's doors first opened in 1918 on the Hill as a market. The original location, which still operates at 1934 Macklind Ave., was built with wood and bricks left over from structures from the 1904 World's Fair and provided staples to the neighborhood as well as a bevy of tasty sandwiches. The space became a dedicated deli in 1980 when the Donley family took over the operation.

Gioia's claim to fame is its hot salami, which makes an appearance on many of the sandwiches on the menu, like the Porknado, Hogfather, Italian Trio and, of course, the flagship Hot Salami sandwich. The original recipe for this succulent sausage was brought over from Northern Italy by founder Charlie Gioia, and the restaurant prepares thousands of pounds of this delicacy in-house every week, slicing it to order while it's still warm.

Gioia's may be just a humble sandwich place, but it has become an icon, not just in St. Louis but across the country. The restaurant has been recognized as one of the best delis in the US by culinary entities like Food Network, Mashed, eater.com, and tastingtable.com. In 2017, Gioia's reached new heights of recognition when the James Beard Foundation bestowed its America's Classic award on the shop.

In addition to the Hill, Gioia's also has locations in Creve Coeur, Valley Park, and Maryland Heights. The deli offers catering services for those who need a hot salami fix for their special event, along with online ordering and shipping for those not fortunate enough to be able to belly up to the counter when the craving hits.

Courtesy of Alex Donley

PROTZEL'S DELICATESSEN

7608 Wydown Blvd. | Clayton | 314.721.4445 | protzelsdeli.com

There used to be a variety of businesses on Wydown Boulevard that served the surrounding tony, tree-lined neighborhoods. At various times a shoe repair shop, a barbershop, and a market, among other establishments, did business along the western end of the boulevard. In time, many of these businesses shuttered, and the area eventually became known for its restaurants. Top-tier eateries like Bistro La Floraison, Wright's Tavern, and Akar, among others, are currently located here. But there are still a few retail holdovers from the old days that continue to ply their trade. One of the longest running and most delicious of these is Protzel's Delicatessen.

Bob and Evelyn Protzel opened Protzel's Deli in 1954. You know how some places have their first dollar posted up by the register? Protzel's has its first salami on display. A proper Jewish deli, this small shop is filled with a whole lot of goodness. Standbys like chopped liver, brisket, and what's been deemed by some the best corned beef in town are available by the pound. There's also a long and varied list of sandwiches to be had here, both classics and specialty creations, in multiple sizes. Basic as I am, I normally default to good ol' pastrami.

Plenty of specialty items are on hand here as well as fresh breads, bagels, matzo, smoked fish, and more. During Passover,

Protzel's is the place to go to prepare for your seder feast, with everything from gefilte fish to potato kugel available.

While I'm not quite old enough to have frequented Protzel's when it was a new spot on the block, I imagine it was pretty much the same as it is now. Nothing fancy, just a few seats for those who choose to nosh on-site, the best deli delights in town, and a line out the door.

MAI LEE

8396 Musick Memorial Dr. | Brentwood | 314.645.2835 | maileestl.com

One of the most beloved restaurants in town, revered by chefs, home cooks, and foodies of all types, Mai Lee is the quintessential American immigrant success story.

After decades of war, Lee Tran left her home in Vietnam in 1978 with her husband and son for a new start in the United States. The family eventually settled in St. Louis, and Tran found work as a server at a number of Chinese restaurants around town to help pay the bills. In 1985 she took the plunge and started Mai Lee with a business partner. At first the restaurant featured a menu of Chinese favorites, and Tran was hesitant to include any Vietnamese food in the bill of fare. But when her partner left her high and dry with a mountain of debt and dim prospects, Tran knew she had to do something to boost business and differentiate Mai Lee from the other Chinese restaurants in town. She decided to change things up, gradually adding some of her favorite dishes from her home country to the menu and becoming St. Louis's first legit Vietnamese restaurant in the process.

Take a peek into the bustling kitchen at Mai Lee and you'll see all manner of pots simmering on the stove, full of the flavors that populate the expansive menu. There are more than 200 dishes to choose from, including flavorful phos, DIY spring rolls, various versions of the local staple St. Paul sandwich, and a plethora of noodle and rice dishes that promise to satisfy any appetite.

In the ensuing years, Mai Lee relocated to a larger space in Brentwood to accommodate its legions of hungry fans, and the restaurant has consistently been honored by the local food press as one of the best in the area. In 2020, Mai Lee got national recognition when it was tapped as a semifinalist for Outstanding Restaurant by the James Beard Foundation.

Courtesy of Mai Lee Restaurant

SHOPS

DON CARLOS

2800 Cherokee St. | 314.773.1707
restaurantji.com/mo/st.-louis/don-carlos-restaurant-

Cherokee Street is home to some of the best Latin American food in town, both restaurants and retailers. I've always been fond of Don Carlos, which is a little bit of both, located right in the middle of this culinary milieu.

As I understand it, the restaurant side is referred to as Don Carlos Restaurant, while the bodega side is Carniceria Latino Americana. From the outside, the restaurant portion looks like someone just tacked a prefab shed onto the side of the main building over the course of a long weekend. But inside this humble structure they serve up a tasty menu of favorites like street tacos, tortas, quesadillas, and burritos the size of a small child's head. Grab-and-go items like guacamole, salsas, and bags of chicherones are on hand if you need something quick. On the weekend, fresh tamales, pork carnitas, beef barbacoa by the pound, and bulk beef menudo are available. Schedule your visit accordingly.

Carniceria Latino Americano is compact but chock-full of all types of goods. Need agave leaves, Mexican Coke,

or an authentic piñata? Look no further. I bought my first bottle of michelada mix here for a Bloody Mary contest I was competing in, and I just kept coming back whenever I needed ingredient inspiration.

There's another Don Carlos location on South Grand Boulevard. It's more of a retail store and less of a restaurant, but it's still a good place to grab some essentials and peruse the carniceria.

OLIVE SUPERMARKET

8041 Olive Blvd. | University City | 314.997.5168
olive-supermarket-inc.mailchimpsites.com

Olive Supermarket has been serving the community since 2006 and is one of the main international markets I hit up when I need to satisfy my urge for esoteric ingredients. With so much in flux along Olive Boulevard these days, like small businesses moving out and large commercial concerns moving in, I often worry about the health and well-being of the area. But then I pop into Olive Supermarket on a Saturday morning—the cars circling the lot looking for parking spaces and the lines stretching to the back of the store make me feel a little bit better about things.

The main market space at Olive Supermarket has aisles full of canned and dry goods, like noodles, teas, a wide array of types of rice, and plenty of sundries like cookware, spirits, and gifty items. The produce section here is always well-stocked with products you're not likely to find in your local grocery, including varieties of daikon, cabbage, mushrooms, and much, much more.

What really sets Olive Supermarket apart from the crowd is its selection of meat and seafood. In the back of the store, customers can browse through a selection of whole ducks, bones for stock, and plenty of off-cuts like chicken necks, beef tripe, and the heart, tongue, and feet of numerous animals. Fully cooked duck, chicken, and pork are also available. On the seafood side, if it swims, Olive Supermarket probably has it. Usual suspects like perch, mackerel, carp, and catfish abound as well as squid, octopus, and eel. With the demise of Seafood City last year, Olive Supermarket has one of the best selections of live seafood that I know of.

INTOXICOLOGY

4321 Manchester Ave. | 314.833.3088 | intoxicologystl.com

Courtesy of Andrew Trinh

The idea for Intoxicology arose from the frustration that owners Andy Foerstel and Melissa Pfeiffer felt when trying to make craft cocktails at home.

"At the time a lot of spirits, ingredients, and bar tools were only available online if at all," said Foerstel. "It was hard to craft a proper cocktail."

Instead of despairing of ever being able to create the ultimate Manhattan, the two took matters into their own hands and opened Intoxicology in 2016.

Located in the historic Grove neighborhood, the shop boasts a carefully curated, ever-evolving roster of more than 500 bottles of spirits and wine. Shelf space at the shop is tight, so customers can be sure that products that make the cut and get a slot are the best of the best. Intoxicology's focus on quality has helped bring some really superior brands to the STL cocktail scene, including Tempus

Fugit and Liber. Many of these tipples are available to sample as well.

Despite the impressive spirits selection, it's important to note that Intoxicology is not a liquor store. If you're looking for a deal on a case of Keystone Light or some bottom-shelf booze for your trash-can punch, move along. The shop is a place of wonder and discovery for those interested in spirits and cocktails. In addition to alcohol, the shop is full of cocktail books; ingredients like shrubs, bitters, and syrups; and even Kold Draft ice. Vintage glassware that Pfeiffer sources from estate sales and antique malls and premium bar tools from brands like Koriko and Barfly are also on hand. Those looking to hone their cocktail skill set can sign up for a variety of classes that are usually held on Thursdays, Fridays, and Saturdays, though be advised these quickly sell out.

Courtesy of Andrew Trinh

THE WINE MERCHANT

9200 Olive Blvd., Ste. 126 | Olivette | 314.863.6282
winemerchantltd.com

Since 1992, the Wine Merchant has been one of the top spots in town to get the best wines, spirits, and assorted other tipples and comestibles. Originally located in Clayton, the Merch's current home is in Olivette, where it relocated in August 2023.

According to owner Jason Main, the secret behind the Wine Merchant's longevity is pretty simple.

"Our guiding principle is we taste and select things that are good," he said. "We are truly a wine merchant. We have great wines at all price points."

Unlike the "stack it high and let it fly" ethos espoused by many wine and spirits retailers, Main and his staff strive to have the best selections in all categories. They taste, mull, and muse as a team, deciding which wines make the cut and get shelf space. They actually travel together to wine country to see firsthand how the vino is made, and while they definitely have strong opinions, they won't volunteer them. If a customer asks for their honest take, though . . .

While wine might be the main attraction at the Merch, there's much more to be discovered there. There's a selection of whiskies that put many whiskey-centric retailers to shame. Plenty of beers, liqueurs, and amaro are also on hand, and the store also has a wide assortment of gourmet goods. There's even a cheesemonger on-site to help customers choose the best bites.

Courtesy of The Wine Merchant

The Wine Merchant also has a multi-tier wine club, with each selection at every level handpicked by Main, so no leftovers and left behinds are being foisted off on members.

The store also recently opened its own on-site bar for those who want to kick back and do some long-form tasting.

JAY INTERNATIONAL FOODS

3172 S Grand Blvd. | 314.772.2552

Like so many others in town, my first exposure to an international grocery store was Jay International Foods. (The awning out front reads Jay while the internet says it's Jay's. Take your pick). It's where I "discovered" my favorite food game, one I now play at most every international grocery that I visit. I pick a random aisle, find something on the shelves without any English on the label, take it home, and figure out what it is and what can be done with it. The resulting culinary adventure isn't always a success, but it's always fun.

Shopping at Jay is different than hitting up a typical grocery store. There are no wine bars, coffee kiosks, gourmet sandwich counters, or anyone hawking samples skewered with frilly toothpicks. Instead of relying on bougie appurtenances to create a shopping "experience," Jay relies on its large and eclectic inventory to keep customers coming back. Jay was the first place in town where I found kimchi that tasted like what I'd had in Korea, and where I discovered wasabi peas, coconut soda, and palm sugar, to name but a few delicacies.

Shopping at Jay can be a challenge at times. Sometimes there's a sign with the name of the country whose flavors are represented in a particular aisle. At other times there's only a picture of a national flag to guide you. There's not always a lot of rhyme or reason to some of the displays, and there may be communication hiccups with the staff, some of whom speak English as a second language. These are minor issues, though, and shouldn't deter anyone from exploring what this culinary institution has to offer. Who knows, you just might find your new favorite thing.

WILD OLIVE PROVISIONS

2201 S 39th St. | 314.300.8089 | wildoliveprovisions.com

Nerida Wilbraham and Scot Martin thought their neighborhood could use a quality wine and cheese store. Instead of complaining about it, they decided to start their own. The husband-and-wife team opened Wild Olive Provisions in 2020, just in time for the pan-

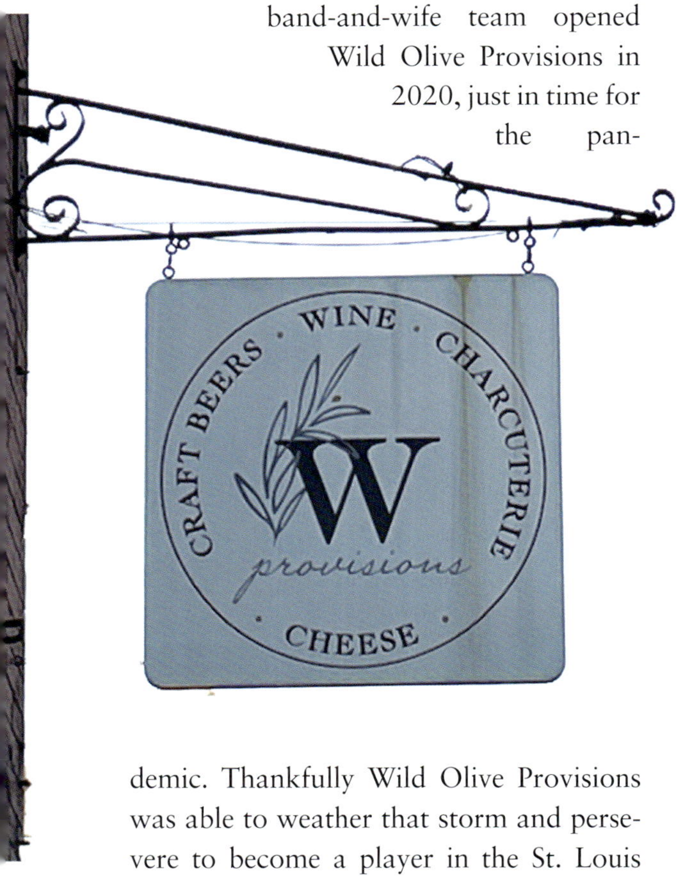

demic. Thankfully Wild Olive Provisions was able to weather that storm and persevere to become a player in the St. Louis wine and specialty food world.

The shop has an eclectic selection of goods, to say the least. Wilbraham said they try to stay away from old-world wines, instead focusing on areas that tend to garner a bit less attention.

The pair have lived in California as well as Wilbraham's native Australia, and accordingly the shop stocks many wines produced in these regions along with vinos from Spain and South Africa. Wilbraham and Martin also taste every wine that they stock before it gets a place on their shelves. There's also a focus at Wild Olive on young, up-and-coming makers, especially women-owned companies, which extends beyond just wine to include other wares like cheeses and craft beer.

While the shop doesn't have a kitchen per se, there are plenty of food options at Wild Olive, including a selection of grab-and-go cheese and charcuterie boxes, fresh bread, and grilled cheese and other sandwiches. Guests can order to-go but are welcome to nosh on-site as well, and there are plenty of by-the-glass wine options to accompany whatever bites they decide on.

The shop has a laid-back afternoon house wine happy hour, and there's always a bottle open to taste for those looking for something new. Wild Olive Provisions also hosts public and private get-togethers, including wine-maker events and wine tastings.

Courtesy of Nerida Wilbraham

EL MORELIA SUPERMERCADO

11982 Paul Mayer Ave. | Bridgeton | 314.209.0014

At first glance, El Morelia Supermercado might appear to be just another big-box store, situated as it is amid similarly large, anonymous retail spaces along St. Charles Rock Road. But the colorful sign over the entrance makes it clear that something special is going on inside.

I first visited El Morelia on a Saturday morning, and the place was buzzing with life, full of patrons of all ages and ethnicities exploring the expansive space. The store moved to its current location, just across the street from the original, in late 2024 and now boasts more square footage than many local grocery stores. The flavors of Latin America are on full display here, with shelves of products hailing from Colombia, Guatemala, Puerto Rico, Mexico, Peru, and the Dominican Republic. As one might expect, there's also a huge selection of agave spirits and plenty of cheesy tchotchkes on hand as well.

While the expanse of products lining the aisles at El Morelia is impressive, it's just the tip of the proverbial iceberg. The periphery of the store's interior is lined with all sorts of specialty departments whipping up fresh, house-made delicacies. There's a tortillaria making fresh tortillas daily and a carneceria that takes up much of the rear of the sales floor and features an enormous case full of prime cuts and a bevy of butchers plying their trade behind it. Meanwhile, a panaderia churns out all sorts of aromatic baked goods. Pan dulce, anyone? There's even an on-site taqueria, Rico's Tacos, that serves up legit street tacos, burritos, and other bites so you can grab a snack while perusing the wares.

El Morelia is an important touchstone for Latinos in St. Louis. With its convenient location, parking for days, and unique offerings, hopefully the store can bring an appreciation of those cultures to the broader community.

LOCAL HARVEST GROCERY

3108 Morgan Ford Rd. | 314.865.5260 | localharvestgrocery.com

I've been frequenting Local Harvest Grocery almost since Maddie Earnest and Patrick Horine opened it in 2007. It was a tiny space with barely enough room for two customers at a time, but almost every square inch was dedicated to local products. Aside from farmers markets, this focus on local was hard to come by back then. In 2011 Local H moved to bigger digs just down Morgan Ford Road, where it remains today. A few days prior to opening, a group of volunteers, myself and my wife among them, formed a human chain in order to transfer all of the inventory to the new space. It was a good time and indicative of the passion this little grocery shop stirs up in its regulars.

Courtesy of Becca

At least 50 percent of goods on the Local Harvest shelves are from within a 150-mile radius of St. Louis, and purveyors and producers set their own prices. The majority of the meat, eggs, and dairy sold there are pasture raised without added hormones or antibiotics, and the majority of the produce is either certified organic or grown under organic conditions. There are also house-made grab-and-go items like sandwiches and wraps available.

Local Harvest hosts a weekly CCSA (Combined Community Supported Agriculture), which offers weekly or bi-weekly pickup of goods sourced from local producers. Local Harvest also champions the cause of limiting food waste wherever possible. The store sells "inglorious" produce—those fruits and veggies that might look rough but are totally edible—at a discount and donates excess to area food banks. Anything left over is composted, never thrown away.

PARKER'S TABLE

7118 Oakland Ave. | Richmond Heights | 314.645.2050 | parkerstable.com

Courtesy of Jonathan Parker

Jonathan Parker knows his way around the food and wine world. After stints as a sommelier, an assistant winemaker, and a wine rep for a local distributor, he began working at a specialty food and wine shop in Clayton. In 1995 he bought the business, changed the name, and eventually moved it to its current location in 2011.

Parker brings his impressive knowledge to bear on his namesake store. He's also staffed it with some of the sharpest folks in the business, so it's hardly surprising that the customer service here is top-notch. The shop is one of those places where I know any recommendation I get from any staff member is going to be squarely on point. Parker likens it to an indie record store where each employee has a genre they're really into and is ready to geek out at a moment's notice. We've been members of the store's Wine of the Month and Cheese of the Month clubs for years (there's a Beer of the Month Club as well). They're great ways to sample new things and get a deal, too.

While wine is certainly front and center here, Parker's Table also carries spirits, beer, and all sorts of specialty foods, from cheese to charcuterie to pasta. There are also sandwiches available, many using Salume Beddu products.

The main shop was originally a post office, and it's slowly morphed over the years into its current form. Parker likes to call it "a nonstop project." In recent years he's taken over the spaces on either side of the main store and opened the Oakland Room, an event space, and the wine-focused Yale Bar.

WORLD MARKET

3900 S Grand Blvd. | 314.351.9495 | www.facebook.com/profile.php?id=100057581343767

Formerly known as Ch Quoc Te International Foods, World Market is located on South Grand, but it's quite a bit south of the culinary and commercial center of that bustling boulevard. Because of this, I think the market gets overlooked in favor of some similar shops in the area. But while it may not be as well known, World Market can more than hold its own with its competitors.

One feature I love to see at international markets is either an adjacent restaurant or a full-service food counter inside so I don't have to drive home on an empty stomach. The World Market space is also home to Joyful House, a Vietnamese restaurant with an expansive menu that includes traditional favorites like pho, bun, and hot pots along with bubble tea and, of all things, full Cajun seafood boils. The restaurant is open Friday through Sunday, but there are usually some grab-and-go options available during the week, and I always take a look at the take-out table when I visit for a bahn mi or some spring rolls.

In addition to aisles of dry and canned goods, World Market has a huge area in the back of the store with seemingly endless stretches of refrigerated shelves of produce and coolers full of meat. There's also a small selection of live seafood.

World Market is a no-frills space, with its concrete floors and fluorescent lights but there's a vibrancy there despite the lack of decor. The store is always full of people of all nationalities when I visit; some are shopping solo, while others browse in chatty clusters. It's a place full of light and activity that really reflects the neighborhood it serves.

BOMBAY BAZAR

1761 Clarkson Rd. | Chesterfield | 636.778.2391 | bbazarstl.com

Those old adages about discovering great things in humble circumstances are so true when it comes to the world of food. There are plenty of restaurants, shops, and markets that fly under the radar here in St. Louis. These businesses are often located in nondescript, crowded developments and rely on the communities they serve to spread the word in lieu of an advertising budget or robust social media presence. A perfect example of this truism is Bombay Bazar. This store serves St. Louis's growing Indian population and anyone who's curious about that country's cuisine and looking for the ingredients to try their hand cooking it at home.

Bombay Bazar, tucked into a nondescript Chesterfield strip mall among the sea of chain retailers, is packed with all of the staples of India. Myriad varieties of lentils, dals, rice, spices, and produce can be found here. In a hurry? There's also a wide selection of frozen Indian foods. My favorite frozen discoveries here include ragda, little mashed-potato cakes that are a popular street food in India, and moong dal kachori, crispy dough balls filled with split mung beans. Bombay Bazar is a prime spot for Indian mangoes when they're in season, and the store also provides supplies needed for celebrations like Diwali, the Hindu festival of lights.

There are few frills at Bombay Bazar, which might put off those who look for more of a spa experience when they shop. For me, though, the austere surroundings make it easier to focus on discovering my next flavor adventure instead of bright and shiny accoutrements.

For Indian expats, Bombay Bazar is a cultural anchor, and for locals it's a gateway to the vibrant culture of India. Make sure to grab a house-made samosa or kachoris, a particularly delicious deep-fried spicy pastry, on the way out.

AO&CO

1641 Tower Grove Ave. | 314.899.0991 | https://bengelina.com/aoco

It usually takes a restaurant, bar, or market a while to get its legs and become a real part of a neighborhood. In my opinion, AO&Co seemed to fit right into the scene in Botanical Heights when it first opened for business in 2019.

I refer to AO&Co as an elevated corner market. It is, in fact, located on a corner (at Tower Grove and McCree Avenues), and the inventory is decidedly upscale—you won't be picking up any toothpaste or cat litter here. However, you can definitely get the makings for your next picnic outing or romantic dinner. A selection of quality wines and spirits shares space with premium coffees and teas, fresh bread, and food items from local favorites like Volpi and Marcoot Creamery as well as popular labels from around the country. There are also tastes from some of owner Ben Poremba's various restaurants, like Olio's much-loved egg salad. There's even a humidor for cigar aficionados. In the back of the store is a café that offers coffee drinks, teas, and chais, as well as a solid menu of sandwiches. There's plenty of outdoor seating to enjoy your purchases too.

Online ordering is also available at AO&Co, though I think checking out the market in person is the way to go. Design-wise, the space is a curious mash-up of

aesthetics. The building itself is a classic South City brick edifice. Inside, many of the shelves and counters are made of rough, unfinished plywood and construction-grade lumber, which contrast nicely with some modern monochromatic fixtures like the black shelving in what I like to call the spirits room. All of these elements work well together to create a low-key, comfortable feel.

ZLATNO ZITO BAKERY & DELI

4573 Gravois Ave. | 314.752.3004

Some places just seem to exist on their own continuum, outside of the hustle and bustle of what passes for modern life. Zlatno Zito Bakery & Deli is one of those sites. The shop is rarely mentioned in print and has almost zero online presence. But when those in the know talk about hidden gems and must-try locations, this Bosnian spot is usually part of the conversation.

Located almost in the shadow of the Bevo Mill, Zlatno Zito is basically two shops in one. On one side is the bakery and deli noted in the name; on the other is a restaurant serving up Bosnian favorites like cevapi and sarma. My experience here has been mostly on the bakery side, though the smells wafting from the kitchen tempt me greatly when I visit.

Truth be told, there isn't much in the way of deli items on the shelves at Zlatno Zito. Some coffees and teas, pickles, a few snacks. The real star of this show is the bakery and the multitude of breads it produces. Zlatno Zito means "golden wheat" in Bosnian, which makes total sense given the racks of bread that line the back of the store. There are so many shapes and sizes of loaves to take in and appreciate. So far, my favorite loaf here has been the lepinja, a traditional pillowy white bread that I just tear into and eat with abandon, often on the drive home.

Both sides of Zlatno Zito are pretty austere, bordering on stark. But while there's not much in the way of decor, the place is full of life. There's always a conversation happening, and plenty of welcoming smiles.

DIGREGORIO'S MARKET

5200 Daggett Ave. | 314.776.1062 | digregoriofoods.com

The Hill is arguably the best-known neighborhood in St. Louis. With its tidy bungalows, quaint shops, and restaurants galore, it's an eminently walkable enclave where it's possible to while away an entire day before you know it. It's also home to perhaps the largest selection of Italian foods in town, and there's no better showcase of these delicacies than DiGregorio's Market.

Salvatore "Sam" DiGregorio opened Di Gregorio's Market in the Hill neighborhood in 1971, and the store quickly became a centerpiece of the neighborhood and the lives of its denizens. Today the name DiGregorio is synonymous with Italian cuisine, both inside and outside the confines of the neighborhood. Now being run by the third generation of the DiGregorio clan, the market is a culinary landmark that attracts customers from all across the metro area and beyond who come to browse the mind-boggling array of meats, cheeses, pastas, olive oils, vinegars, wines, and much more that fill the shelves.

DeGregorio's selection of Italian goods from regional, national, and international producers, including local favorites like Volpi, is impressive to say the least. But DiGregorio's is equally well known for its almost overwhelming array of house-made delicacies. A short list of these includes myriad sauces, olive salad, spiedinis, cannolis, salsiccia, multiple meatball variations, and even frozen pizza and microwaveable lasagna and pasta dinners for those who don't have the time or inclination to spend all day in the kitchen. The store even has parmesan that's grated on-site.

Courtesy of DiGregorio's Market

The Hill is all about community, and one has only to stop by DiGregorio's on a busy Saturday morning and see that community out in force.

VOM FASS

7314 Manchester Rd. | Maplewood | 314.932.5262 | vomfassusa.com

Anita von Ballmoos came to the US from her native Switzerland to pursue a romance with her now-husband, Joe Stach. She ended up not only gaining a spouse but starting a successful one-of-a-kind business in Vom Fass.

Vom Fass is a German company, and von Ballmoos's St. Louis franchise, which opened in 2009, is one of only a handful of stores left in the States in the wake of COVID. Its primary mission is selling the highest-quality oils and vinegars as well as a wide selection of liqueurs and spirts, many of which are available only at the shop. Vom Fass means "of the cask" in German, and that's what makes the business so unique. Customers can get samples of almost everything in the store, including booze, before they take the plunge and make a purchase. Not sure about going all in on that 25-year-old Armagnac, or wondering if that aged

Courtesy of Luke Johnson

balsamic is really all it's cracked up to be? Try before you buy. Brilliant. In addition to its liquid products, Vom Fass also carries a selection of spices, sauces, pastas, and other boutique food items as well as wines.

While the Vom Fass products are unique and most definitely delicious, von Ballmoos also hosts myriad events at the shop, showcasing some of the ingredients available as well as the talents of local chefs, sommeliers, and assorted purveyors. Dinners, wine tastings, and classes happen almost weekly, and many have developed strong followings. A prime example are the authentic Swiss raclette dinners held several times a year. These events, where guests cook their own cheesy, meaty feast at their table, almost immediately sell out when tickets go live.

Vom Fass's tagline is "The Candy Store for Grown-Ups," which aptly describes the inventory and also explains the smiles on customers' faces when they enter this world of flavor.

FOREST & MEADOW HERB SHOP AND CLINIC

3232 Ivanhoe Ave. | 314.553.9777 | forestandmeadow.com

I discovered Forest & Meadow Herb Shop and Clinic by chance when I was asked to come up with a cocktail for a demo at the Taste of Missouri Market. Forest & Meadow owner Amanda Jokerst, who was also participating in the event, hooked me up with some of her chai tea, which I made into a syrup. The drink went over extremely well, and since then I've looked to the shop when I need ingredients to inspire me.

Jokerst found her herbal passion by accident. She was studying sociology and just happened to pick up a book on what to do in case of a societal collapse. Herbal medicine was mentioned, and the idea so intrigued her that she switched gears and signed up for an online herb class. Jokerst eventually became a certified clinical herbalist and began a clinical practice in 2017. After testing the retail waters at the Schlafly Bottleworks farmers market, she took the plunge and opened her own brick-and-mortar shop.

Courtesy of Amanda Jokers

I gravitate toward the shop's teas, bitters, and shrubs for cocktails and cooking, and Forest & Meadow creation have found their way onto several loca restaurant menus. But the company is als

Courtesy of Amanda Jokerst

an apothecary and clinic promoting wellness through herbs. Most everything in the shop with a Forest & Meadow label on it is made in small batches in-house, from dried herbs to tinctures. Forest & Meadow products can also be found around town at Local Harvest Grocery (localharvestgrocery.com/lhg), Union Studio (stlunionstudio.com), Health On Main (optimanutrition.net), and the Procure Shop by the Women's Creative (shopprocure.com). Jokerst even hopes to have a canned nonalcoholic beverage available soon-ish.

HAN LAO

7219 Manchester Rd. | Maplewood | 314.932.1354

I have long been fascinated with Japanese konbini. These convenience stores, which also stock the usual groceries and household items, are known for also having delicious grab-and-go food of all types. Some of these shops are much revered and have almost cult status. I've yet to make it to Japan to check out the konbini scene there, but Han Lao in Maplewood has satisfied my desire for now.

Han Lao is owned by the same folks that own Robata across the street, which specializes in ramen, sushi, and yakitori. They used to have a well-regarded Thai/Laotian restaurant with the Han Lao name in Brentwood that closed during COVID. At one point I heard that the plan was to reopen the restaurant, but the owners decided to relocate and reimagine the concept while keeping the familiar moniker. Han Lao has plenty of Asian groceries on hand, from rice and noodles to a really impressive array of sake. The inventory also includes housewares and sundries. For those who can't make it to one of the larger international grocery stores in the city or out west, Han Lao is a convenient option.

The big draw at Han Lao for me, though, is the food. I depend on them to satisfy the cravings for chicken yakisoba that come over me every so often. I also highly recommend the Spam musobi, that snack-time favorite that's a lot like Japanese onigiri, with a piece of my favorite canned meat placed on top of rice and wrapped in nori. Lucky for me, Han Lao is within walking distance from my house, so it's easy for me to get my fix.

SOULARD FARMERS MARKET

730 Carroll St. | facebook.com/SoulardMarket

I think of Soulard Farmers Market as sort of an under-the-radar St. Louis icon. It's been around since 1779 and takes up a big chunk of real estate, yet I don't often hear it referred to by the foodie set. However, I believe the market is a real jewel and an important part of the city experience.

I remember going on field trips to the market when I was a kid. At that time I'd mostly eaten canned veggies, and the sight of row upon row of vibrantly colored produce made quite the impression on me. Most farmers markets in these parts are held on a weekly schedule in a park, parking lot, or some other public space that functions as something else the rest of the time. What I like about Soulard Market is that it is housed in its own building and so has hours during the week as well. However, it is at its bustling best on Saturdays, when all of the stalls are full and people-watching is at peak levels. Unlike some other area markets, Soulard features vendors selling fresh meat and seafood along with the usual fruits and vegetables.

The red brick heart of the market dates to about 1929, and it's probably my favorite part of the space. It houses some permanent fixtures, including the Cajun Corner bar, which serves up potent Irish coffees and Bloody Marys for those who like to imbibe as they shop. Indoor bathrooms are also a plus. After shopping, take advantage of being in the heart of one of St. Louis's most historic neighborhoods. Take a walk, check out the gorgeous architecture, and pop into one of the multitude of bars, restaurants, coffee shops, and boutiques that line the surrounding blocks.

GLOBAL FOODS MARKET

421 N Kirkwood Rd. | Kirkwood | 314.835.1112 | globalfoodstl.com

Courtesy of Global Foods

Many people put up barriers that keep them from venturing out of their comfort zone. I find this to be especially true when it comes to food. Despite the fact that noshing on something new presents no risk, it can be a real chore to get someone to try something outside of their bubble, even if they're curious about it. Global Foods Market, though, makes it easy for shoppers to expand their horizons.

Global Foods is a fantastic entry point for those who are interested in exploring world cuisines but keep falling back on lame excuses as to why they never seem to get around to it. The store is conveniently located in the heart of Kirkwood, so it's easy to find. There's plenty of parking. The store is bright, roomy, and accessible. The aisles have plenty of signage and are a cinch to navigate. In addition to food from all over the world, the shelves are also well stocked with day-to-day household goods so shoppers don't have to make a special trip to another store for their staples. They can pick up their bread, milk, and eggs along with the unfamiliar cuts of meat, exotic produce, and brightly colored bags of snacks that have piqued their interest. Can't find what you're looking for? The folks at Global are more than happy to track it down and order it.

I really wish this store had been around when I was growing up in Kirkwood in the 1970s and 1980s. Who knows, maybe I would've thrown off my suburban yoke and started expanding my palate much sooner than I actually did.

Courtesy of Global Foods

WORLDWIDE INTERNATIONAL FOOD MARKET

7238 N Lindbergh Blvd. | Hazelwood | 314.731.3500

The section of North Lindbergh on the way to Worldwide International Food Market is not a particularly scenic route. The road is a seemingly endless stretch of anonymous, squat, monolithic buildings with no discernible purpose—just big gray boxes. Then there's a little splash of color. Turns out it's the Hazelwood DMV. But the market is next door, so the DMV makes a good landmark to keep an eye out for. Otherwise there's not much except some faded letters on the facade and a few shopping carts in front to let you know you've arrived.

While the outside of the market is nondescript, inside it's hard to know where to focus, because there's so much

to look at and take in. The aisles are wide, so there's plenty of elbow room to browse. The market has a fairly small selection of foods from Asia and other areas around the world, but the main focus at World International Food Market is Middle Eastern goods. The store is known for its variety of halal meats and fresh pita bread. There's also a surprisingly large selection of candy and sweets here, along with pastries and baked goods from Tanoor Bakery in Hickory Hills, Illinois. The market is also a key source of goods for celebrations like Ramadan.

Unlike some independent markets, Worldwide International Food Market updates its Facebook page regularly, so it's easy to keep abreast of specials and what's in and out of stock. While it's not in the food realm, make sure to check out the hookah section when you visit. I have never seen so many hookah pipes, tobaccos, and accessories all in one place.

OTHER PURVEYORS

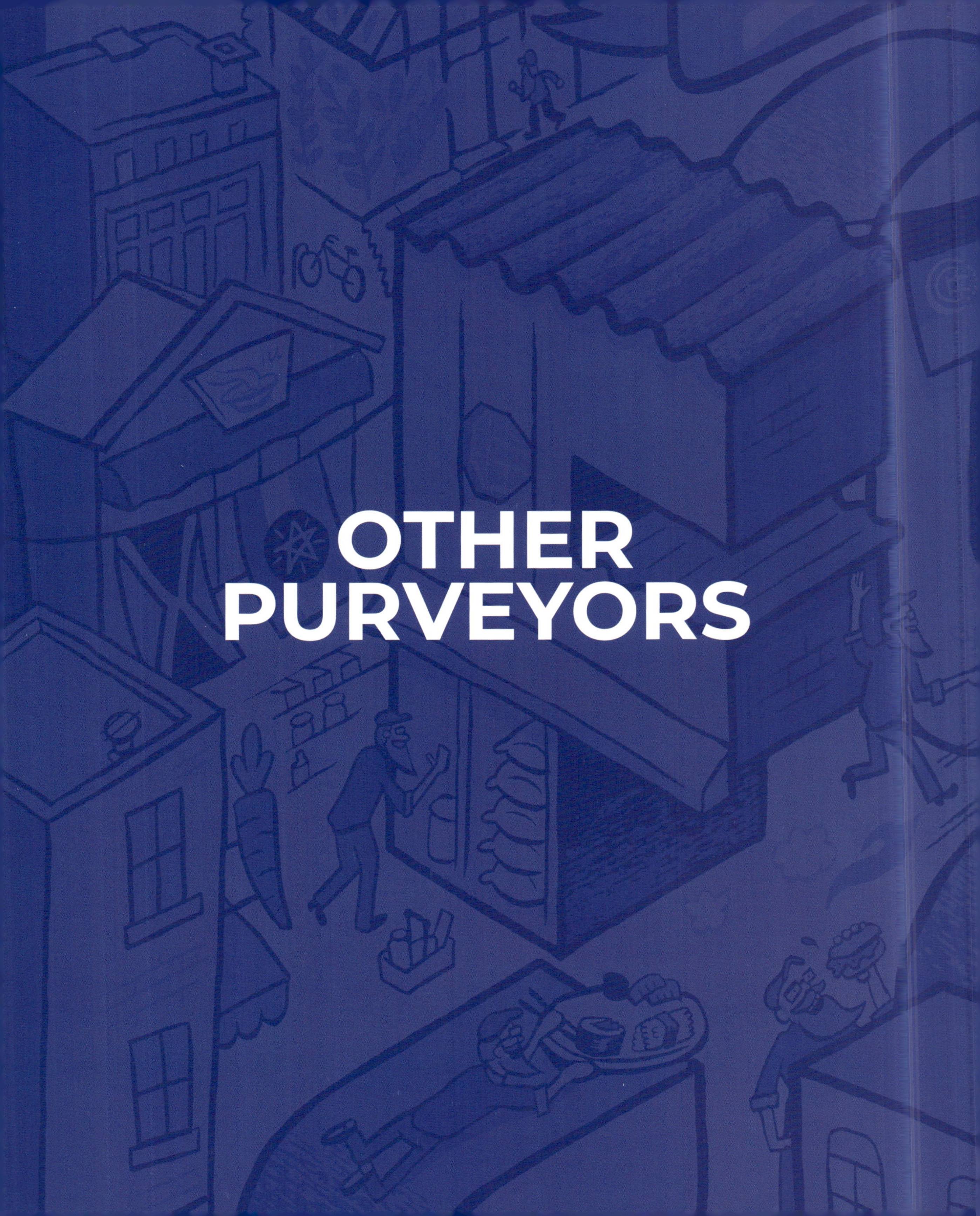

PIERCE CREEK CATTLE COMPANY

10405 Old Olive Rd. | Creve Coeur | piercecreekcattlecompany.com

Knowing where your food comes from is important, and for St. Louisans who care about the source of their meat, buying from Pierce Creek Cattle Company in Lonedell, is the way to go.

Owners Kent Evans and Rachelle L'Ecuyer took over the farm, which has been in Evans's family since 1943, in 2017. The land hadn't hosted bovines in a decade or so, but after looking into a variety of crops they could possibly plant, the pair decided to give the cows another shot.

The farm consists of 240 acres, roughly half of which are chemical-free pasture land that provides the main source of food for the herd. Pierce Creek cows are then grain-finished and receive no added hormones, steroids, or unnecessary antibiotics. When the time comes, the cows are processed locally as well, so curious carnivores can see the exact trajectory of the beef from pasture to plate. Pierce Creek supplies meat to numerous area restaurants, including Barrio, Sasha's on Shaw, and Sasha's on DeMun. In addition, fans can find Pierce Creek smash burgers at local events courtesy of the farm's food truck, dubbed the MOObile.

Home cooks can pick up Pierce Creek beef at the company's recently opened brick-and-mortar location (also known as Pierce Creek) in Creve Coeur, which used to house Kohn's Kosher Deli. The space also boasts a bakery, a deli, a butcher shop, and a locally focused market. Pierce Creek beef is also available at the Wine Merchant as well as online. Customers with some freezer space can order quarter, half, or whole beef packages as well, and five smaller packages ranging from 17 to 34 pounds are also available.

Courtesy of Rachelle L'Ecuyer

NARROW GAUGE BREWING COMPANY

1545 N US Hwy 67 | Florissant | 314.501.6108 | narrowgaugestl.shop

Jeff Hardesty took his homebrewing hobby and went pro in 2016, opening Narrow Gauge Brewing Company inside Cugino's Italian Eatery (cuginosflorissant.com) in Florissant. He put his background as a mechanical engineer to use to convert an unused basement banquet room into a brewing facility that has gone on to produce some of the most and tasty creative beers around.

Courtesy of Jeff Hardesty

Narrow Gauge made its name crafting New England–style IPAs, a hazy, juicy variant. This style remains the brewery's go-to, with brews like Fallen Flag and OJ Run continuing to be sales leaders. Hardesty and his wife, Heather, built the brand the old-school way, traveling to beer events all over the country and letting the beers do the talking. For a long while Narrow Gauge brews could only be purchased at Cugino's, but these days they can be found on store shelves across Missouri and Illinois.

In 2023 Hardesty moved the operation to a new production facility just a few doors down from Cugino's in a former swimming pool store. A tasting room followed in 2024 with 75 seats and 24 taps split between old standbys and new favorites. There's no kitchen on-site, but guests can order food from Cugino's via QR code or bring in other eats.

In addition to producing award-winning beers, Narrow Gauge has also emerged as a community cornerstone. The brewery is named after the narrow-gauge railway that once connected Florissant and St. Louis City, and like its namesake, it's helped bring new visitors to this oft-overlooked municipality. Despite the brewery's success, Hardesty doesn't plan on Narrow Gauge becoming a brewing behemoth.

"We always wanted to be more of a boutique craft brewer," he said. "We want to focus on quality instead of chasing a number."

STILL 630

1000 S Fourth St. | 314.513.2275 | still630.com

Courtesy of David Weglarz

David Weglarz had done some home brewing and had seen how craft beer had exploded on the beverage scene. Being a whiskey aficionado, he thought craft spirits could have a similar trajectory and so embarked on a journey of distillation.

Weglarz set up shop in St. Louis, partly due to the town's attractive liquor regs, but there was also a deeply personal reason—it's his wife Sidni's hometown. To honor his new home, Weglarz named his venture StilL 630. The St and L represent the city's initials, while the 630 stands for 630 feet, the height and the width of the iconic St. Louis Arch.

StilL 630's first products, Rally Point rye whiskey and its un-aged counterpart Big Jake, debuted in 2013. The distillery's focus is still whiskey, but a wide variety of spirits are now crafted there, from gin to rum to apple brandy. These days StilL 630 produces seven core spirits all year round plus numerous seasonal and annual releases and collaborations, like the gin it recently made for 21c Museum Hotel. In 2026 StilL 630 plans to commemorate the 250th anniversary of the founding of the United States by releasing a single-barrel bourbon each month to spotlight various milestones in the country's history.

All of this creativity hasn't gone unnoticed. Since its inception the distillery has won numerous awards and accolades for its spirits, including multiple Best of Category nods from the American Distilling Institute.

The distillery offers tours on Saturdays by appointment. On Fridays, fans can step up to StilL 630's bar and order a cocktail from a monthly rotating menu and also get a taste of experimental batches of spirits still in the works.

DAMN FINE HAND PIES

4000 Shaw Blvd. | damnfinehandpies.com

Damn Fine Hand Pies debuted as a purveyor at Tower Grove Farmers' Market in the summer of 2021 and soon had some of the longest lines there waiting for their hand pies, sourdough bread, doughnuts, and other baked delights.

The little bakery that could started as the dream of Madeline Hissong, a culinary school grad who worked in several high-profile kitchens in Chicago and St. Louis. Inspired by the pies her great-grandmother made during her childhood, she turned her attention to baking, honing her skills at local favorite Knead Bakehouse before starting Damn Fine. She then partnered with Gene Bailey, himself a restaurant industry vet who consulted for and worked front-of-the-house at local eateries like Juniper and Rooster. Bailey helped take Hissong's original vision and expand the business. Damn Fine finally outgrew the confines of the farmers market, and in the summer of 2024 the duo opened up a brick-and-mortar location in the Shaw neighborhood.

I first met Hissong and Bailey at a pop-up they held at a bar where I worked. One bite of that first glazed brioche donut and I was hooked. The duo's passion and dedication was evident in the flavor and consistency of that humble donut, which remains one of my favorites from any bakery in town. On the hand pie front, the sausage and gravy pie is a portable masterpiece of flavor that shouldn't be missed, and if a loaf of their sourdough bread is available when you visit, don't hesitate. You need it.

Hissong and Bailey still source locally from some of their farmers market colleagues, ensuring the best ingredients and there are plenty of vegan options available as well. You can also grab a hand pie at their concession at Energizer Park, home of St. Louis City SC.

DAMN FINE
HAND PIES

BIG HEART TEA CO.

2618 Winnebago St. | 314.875.0040 | bighearttea.com

Founder Lisa Govro started Big Heart Tea in 2012, originally selling her wares out of an old converted camper trailer at area farmers markets and other local events. That trailer still sits outside Big Heart Tea headquarters, a monument to the company's humble beginnings.

These days, Big Heart has outgrown the trailer and then some. The brand has been endorsed by media heavyweights like Oprah Winfrey and the *New York Times*, and it's available at national chains like World Market and select Whole Foods locations in the Midwest and Rocky Mountain regions, along with plenty of mom-and-pop retailers. Big Heart has a signature line of about 15 tried-and-true teas at any one time and introduces a couple of new varieties each year to see if they'll prove popular enough to become part of the regular roster. Cup of Sunshine is the first Big Heart tea I ever tried, a spicy mix of

golden turmeric and ginger, and it remains the one I reach for most often.

While Big Heart teas certainly are tasty and top-shelf, the company itself is also something special. Everything the company does is thoughtful and intentional. Big Heart only uses the best ethically sourced tea, and it's packaged it in sustainable and biodegradable materials like compostable non-GMO sugarcane and conflict-free wood pulp.

Govro said she thinks of Big Heart as more of a "love note company than a tea company," which has a special resonance in this age of faceless corporate entities. Big Heart's teas aren't just beverages but inspiration for discussions about self care, community, and wellness. Plus they just make you feel good, inside and out.

SALUME BEDDU

314.942.6300 | salumebeddu.com

Mark Sanfilipo, owner of Salume Beddu, began his love affair with Italian cured meats in, of all places, Germany. While he was a student at the University of Stuttgart he tasted elk sausage brought back by an Italian exchange student, an experience that turned his head and then some. A later stint working as a cook at Nancy Silverton's Pizzeria Mozza in Los Angeles exposed him to just what a cured meat program could be.

Sanfilipo returned to St. Louis in the mid-2000s and began trying his hand at making his own sausages and selling them at local farmers markets. He opened a brick-and-mortar space in 2010, offering a range of meats, sandwiches, and sundry retail items as well as serving as the company's production shop. He moved the operation to a converted egg roll factory in 2015 and began focusing on wholesale.

Despite its ever-growing popularity (*Forbes* magazine famously declared the company's salami the best in the country), Salume Beddu's production numbers remain relatively small, with an unwavering focus on quality that starts with procuring the best ingredients and continues through the entire butchering and curing process.

Salume Beddu, which translates to "beautiful cured meat" in Sicilian, produces approximately 10 different salami at any one time, plus other items when possible. The company has its products in more than 20 STL-area Schnuck's stores now, plus various local wine and spirits shops, boutique groceries, and CSAs, as well as online via the company website. Fans of the sandwiches that the original location served up can still get their fix at Parker's Table (parkerstable.com).

SALUME BEDDU
Saint Louis
ARTISAN CURED MEATS
CALABRESE
CALABRESE BRAND SALAME:
our calabrian style salame is spicy and bold flavored with dried chiles, smoked paprika, coriander, wine and garlic.
FINOCCHIONA
FINOCCHIONA BRAND SALAME:
simple and straightforward, our tuscan style salame is flavored with toasted fennel, black pepper, garlic, and red wine.
VENETO
VENETO BRAND SALAME:
based on the veneto's spice trade history, our veneto salame is complex with a strong depth of flavor comprised of a medieval spice blend including cinnamon, nutmeg, cardamom, and a host of other spices.
CRESPONE
CRESPONE BRAND SALAME:

STRINGBEAN COFFEE COMPANY

858 Hanley Industrial Court | 314.472.3267 | stringbeancoffee.com

Pete Cohen started roasting coffee in 2011 for his own use after becoming dissatisfied with the bitter takeout java he was forced to imbibe. Crafting coffee was also a way to deal with his unfulfilling career as a commercial banker and the death of his wife. Soon his hobby became a business, and Cohen began live roasting and selling his coffee at area farmers markets. In short order, demand grew and Cohen left the world of finance behind to bring his smooth, sustainable coffee, dubbed Stringbean, to a thirsty populace.

The name of the company is a nod to two of Cohen's passions, coffee and music (think guitar strings). Stringbean's first commercially available coffee was Redeye Roast, an espresso blend that remains one of the brand's best sellers. The stable of products has grown to include eight coffees, and the company has its coffee in around 80 locations in three states, from large grocery stores to small local concerns like Local Harvest Grocery and Parker's Table. A subscription service is also available.

Cohen is not just committed to producing a quality cuppa joe; he's also a dedicated social justice advocate. Stringbean is part of the Cafe Femenino Foundation, a nonprofit organization that provides support to women and families in coffee-producing communities around the world. The company is Fair Trade and Rainforest Alliance certified and encourages customers to return their used coffee bags for reuse. Cohen also uses the

Swiss Water Process, a 100-percent chemical-free decaffeination procedure, to create his decaf roasts.

Despite Stringbean's steady growth, Cohen continues to keep things simple. He roasts his own beans by hand, without computers or automated assistance, under a disco ball that was used on the set of the original *Soul Train*. Of course, there's always music playing.

Courtesy of Stringbean

CLEMENTINE'S NAUGHTY & NICE CREAMERY

multiple locations | clementinescreamery.com

Ice cream has long been part of Tamara Keefe's life. She began making ice cream with her family with a garage-sale ice cream maker and in the process built a community of fans among her neighbors. Though she would go on to enter the corporate world, eventually becoming a senior brand manager for a major nutrition company, the experience of community and comfort she got from those homemade ice cream sessions never left her. In 2014, burned out, she left behind the rat race and returned to her roots, starting her own ice cream company, Clementine's Naughty & Nice Creamery.

Clementine's is a microcreamery, which means they craft their ice cream by hand in small batches. There are no artificial ingredients used, and the final product has between 16 and 18 percent butterfat, so it's way heavier and denser than ice cream made by large commercial concerns. The Naughty in the company name refers to Clementine's line of boozy ice cream, infused with alcohol via a proprietary method that leaves the ice cream with a decided kick.

Courtesy of Clementine's Ice Cream

Clementine's currently has eight shops, and its ice cream is available for online ordering via Goldbelly, with local delivery offered on a variety of ordering platforms.

Courtesy of Clementine's Ice Cream

I usually frequent Clementine's Clayton location in the DeMun neighborhood, as it's within a reasonable distance of my house and lets me walk off some of my indulgence. Nothing better than strolling to the shop on a summer evening for a couple of scoops of Salted Cracker Caramel or Gooey Butter Cake.

THE BIG O

drinkthebigo.com

I met the husband-and-wife team of Bill Foster and Kathy Kuper in 2012 at a tasting event, about a year or so after they began producing the Big O ginger liqueur. I was taken with their passion and energy, and their sublime spirited creation quickly became one of my go-to ingredients for creating cocktails.

Foster and Kuper were initially inspired to craft their own liqueur by some homemade lemoncello they sampled during a trip to London. They came up with an ultrasmooth combination of ginger and other spices that garnered positive reviews from family and friends who tried it. In true entrepreneurial fashion, they decided to bring their vision to the thirsty masses.

The Big O is based on a vodka and an eau de vie, both distilled in Southern Missouri. It's then infused with fresh hand-chopped ginger and assorted proprietary ingredients. About 500 pounds of ginger is used per batch. I've helped chop some of that ginger before, and I can attest that it takes a good while to get a batch's worth.

The resulting libation is full and round with depth to spare. Unlike, say, sushi ginger, the Big O isn't harsh or sharp, just warm and enveloping. The Big O is great to just sip on, but when used as a cocktail ingredient it lifts drinks into another realm. One of my favorite ways to employ the Big O is to use it as a replacement for simple syrup in an old-fashioned for a subtly complex riff on that classic.

After 14 years, the Big O is still very much a family affair. Foster and Kuper still do all of the heavy lifting themselves, and their son, Chris Foster, produces videos for the brand and handles social media duties.

Courtesy of Christopher Foster

Courtesy of Christopher Foster

TWO MEN AND A GARDEN

twomenandagarden.com

Brett Tintera and Joel Austin turned a shared hobby into one of St. Louis's best-known local brands, Two Men and a Garden. The journey began in 2006 when the two neighbors decided to combine the bounty of their prolific backyard gardens. In short order they had more produce than they knew what to do with. So they took the excess, tweaked a couple of family recipes, and began making salsa and pickles.

"We never sat there and said, 'Let's make this a commercial venture,'" Austin said. "Our whole goal was to make enough money for a new tiller for the garden."

It wasn't long, though, before the Two Men and a Garden brand outgrew that goal and was ready for the big time. The company's products debuted on area store shelves in 2010. Currently the brand is in some 2,000 stores, including various Schnucks, Dierbergs, Whole Foods, Wal-Mart, and Winn-Dixie locations, along with several smaller places in all 50 states. The duo have also leveraged their pickle prowess by partnering with the St. Louis Shock, St. Louis's pro pickleball team, to promote the sport by putting the team logo and info on Two Men and a Garden delivery vehicles and packaging.

Courtesy of Two Men and a Garden

The company now offers nine salsas, six pickles, and five DIY pickling pouches along with a variety of pickle spears. At the time I'm writing this, Two Men is also working on a collaboration with another St. Louis institution, Old Vienna, to come up with a Red Hot Riplets spicy dill pickle chip. This quintessential local brand continues to grow and evolve, and I can't wait to see what they come up with next.

SIDE PROJECT BREWING

7458 Manchester Rd. (brewery) | Side Project Cellar (bar) 7373 Marietta Ave. | Side Project Pizza 2657 Lyle Ave. | Maplewood | sideprojectbrewing.com

Side Project Brewing sold its very first beer in 2013, and since then this microbrewery has established itself as one of the top breweries in the country. The name refers to the company's origin as a "side project" while co-owner Cory King worked as head brewer for Perennial Artisan Ales, another top-tier local brewery. While it may have started out as an incidental affair, Side Project has become very much its own thing and a major force in the local and national beer communities.

King and his wife, Karen, initially started Side Project as an exclusively oak-aged brewery with a concentration on Belgian-style beers, though these days they do put out some other styles like lagers and IPAs. For those interested in getting into some of the more esoteric styles, like sours and farmhaus ales, look no further.

The Kings opened Side Project Cellar in 2014, just a few blocks away from the brewery, to showcase their creations as well as some of their favorite beers and whiskies from other producers. In the ensuing years the Cellar has garnered its own set of

Courtesy of Tim Bottchen

accolades as a beer bar that pours and presents its beers properly. In 2016 Side Project added a full-fledged tasting room to the brewery proper, and in 2025 it opened its own pizza place, Side Project Pizza (duh), just across the street.

Outside the brewery, Side Project beers are available at a handful of area restaurants and a couple of retailers. They usually sell out immediately upon release, so those in the know take advantage of La Coterie, a membership program whose members get first crack at reserving and purchasing new brews.

EARTHDANCE ORGANIC FARM SCHOOL

233 S Dade Ave. | Ferguson | 314.521.1006 | earthdancefarms.org

EarthDance Organic Farm School began in 2008 on a single acre of leased land in Ferguson. Since then, Molly Rockamann Korte, EarthDance's founder and CEO, and her team of passionate agriculturists have built a farm that produces the highest-quality produce possible and provides important educational resources to the community.

The farm produces myriad crops all year long, from radishes and rhubarb in the spring to carrots and tomatoes in the summer to squash in the fall. This bounty can be enjoyed in dishes at St. Louis–area restaurants like Vicia (viciarestaurant.com) and purchased locally at Local Harvest Grocery (localharvestgrocery.com), City Greens Market (stlcitygreens.org), and Ferguson Farmers Market (fergusonfarmersmarket.com), among others. In keeping with its mission of supporting the community and making sure clean food is accessible to everyone, EarthDance hosts a pay-what-you-can farm stand housed in a converted toolshed on the farm that sells fresh produce based on what the individual customer can afford.

In addition to growing and selling ethical and sustainable food, EarthDance also offers much-needed education on all things agricultural. Some of the programs the farm supports include Spring Training for Gardeners, which began in 2021 and teaches the basics of growing your own food via in-person and online classes. EarthDance has also partnered with the Ferguson-Florissant School District to provide students with a variety of unique agricultural experiences like school gardens, apprenticeships, and visits from the farm's mobile kitchen, appropriately dubbed the Freshmobile. Additional educational opportunities are available at the Farm Stand, including cooking demos, monthly story time for kids and families, and pay-what-you-can yoga classes. EarthDance recently went solar with the addition of 72 solar panels that power the farm, and extra power generated is donated to the community.

Courtesy of Jess Coffin

NATHANIEL REID BAKERY

11243 Manchester Rd. | Kirkwood | 314.858.1019 | nrbakery.com

Courtesy of Whitney Ostercamp

In a small storefront in a Kirkwood strip mall, Chef Nathaniel Reid crafts world-class baked goods with little flash but consummate skill.

Reid graduated from Le Cordon Bleu in Paris and plied his trade in top pastry kitchens around the world, including the three-Michelin-star Restaurant de Joel Robuchon in Las Vegas, before returning to his home state of Missouri and opening his eponymous shop in 2016. His creations have been heralded on forums from Food Network to *Travel & Leisure*, and he was a semifinalist for the James Beard Best Baker: Midwest award in 2019 and 2020 and got a semifinal nod for Best Bakery in 2025.

Perusing the cases at Reid's is like getting a peek at the inner workings of this master chef's mind. There are a plethora of sweet and savory items, like croissants, cookies, and financiers; a dozen different macarons; and decadent pastries. My favorite of the pastry options is the jarmo, a pistachio almond cake topped with a raspberry confit and pistachio mousseline. There's also a small but tasty list of sandwiches and quiches available.

Reid could get his creations on any menu and on any shelves in town, but he chooses to sell his goods exclusively at his own shop. Limited supply means outsized demand, and lines out the door are a fairly common occurrence. However, you'll never see so many people queued up for anything with so many smiles on their faces anywhere else. The jewellike colors and incredible textures have young and old alike pressing their faces against the glass trying to take it all in. Social media mavens take note, everything on display is imminently Instagrammable if that's your thing.

1220 SPIRITS

1220spirits.com

According to 4 Hands Brewing Co. owner and founder Kevin Lemp, distilling spirits was never part of the original plan when he opened the brewery in 2011. But with the explosion of craft breweries in the past decade or so, he started looking around for a way to diversify the company's offerings and give the salesforce something to sink its teeth into. Enter 1220 Spirits.

The 1220 brand debuted in 2018 with Origin, a botanically complex New American–style gin. The company eventually added additional spirits to the mix, including Encryption vodka, Spetra Amaro, Flora Aperitif, and Withered Oak whiskies, among others. The company also has a line of canned cocktails that are more than just fizzy monochromatic fruit punches. These drinks put fresh ingredients like ginger, lavender, and pineapple to the forefront with very tasty results. I suggest trying a side-by-side comparison with your favorite premixed libation and experiencing the difference.

What I most appreciate about the 1220 line is the curiosity and open-mindedness behind it. Like many distilleries, 1220 could have focused on easy cash grabs like candy-flavored vodkas or a prefab whiskey with a carefully scripted Prohibition backstory. Instead, the company opted to innovate and not be beholden to what the competition deems to be the norm. In addition to having its spirits featured in cocktails at bars across town, 1220 has also collaborated with area icons like Vicia, Brasserie, and the Missouri Botanical Garden to create custom versions of Origin Gin for each of them. Creativity is 1220's watchword, and it shows in every drop that comes off the still.

Courtesy of Heidi Stehr

4 HANDS BREWING CO.

4 Hands Brewery & Tasting Room | 1220 S 8th St. | 4handsbrewery.com

Courtesy of Heidi Stehr

4 Hands Brewing Co. was part of the craft beer wave that hit the St. Louis area in the mid-2000s and includes Urban Chestnut Brewing Company, 2nd Shift Brewing Company, Civil Life Brewing Company, and Perennial Artisan Ales. Founder Kevin Lemp had been working in the beverage industry on the sales and marketing side of things, fell in love with the craft beer category, and decided to take the plunge and start his own brewery.

4 Hands brewed its first beer, Cast Iron Oatmeal Brown, on 11/11/2011, and never looked back. From that first batch a brand was born, and in 2025 there were 12 core and 22 seasonal and specialty releases from 4 Hands, making it one of the biggest craft breweries in town.

I have always been impressed with 4 Hands's taproom game. The brewery was one of the first that I can remember teaming up with a quality culinary partner (originally Peacemaker Lobster & Crab Co., now Hi-Pointe Drive-In) to create its food menu. Over the years the tasting room has expanded to the second floor of the building where another full bar awaits, plus arcade games and plenty of seating. In addition to the original taproom, these days 4 Hands also has locations in the District in Chesterfield, downtown Kirkwood, and a space at Lambert International Airport, all offering their own food and drink menus.

I'm also a sucker for places that give back, and philanthropy is a key component to 4 Hands's success. To this end the company created City Wide, a beer and give-back initiative. Each year the brewery partners with four local nonprofits and donates a portion of every case of City Wide beer sold. So far, 4 Hands has put about $350,000 back into the community.

OLD VIENNA RED HOT RIPLETS

oldviennallc.com

I'm an aficionado of salty, crunchy snacks. I'll give any crisp, chip, nugget, or wafer a try at least once. But the one I always come back to is Old Vienna Red Hot Riplets.

In 1936, a visionary named Louis Kauffmann began selling potato chips in St. Louis under the name Old Vienna. Ownership has changed many times since then, and the company was kaput for a bit before starting back up in the 1990s, but Kauffmann's legacy lives on. These days the company has a full line of snacks, spicy and otherwise, but the flagship Red Hot Riplets remains my favorite, and the one potato chip I esteem above all others.

According to the Old Vienna website, the chips have "advanced ridge technology" that serves to hold the proprietary piquant seasoning in place. I really love the thought of a group of scientists huddled in a secret South City lab developing this tasty tech. Ridges aside, it's the seasoning that makes this snack so irresistible. The first bite is sweet, then the flavor segues into a slowly building heat that at times threatens to overwhelm the palate, before slowly ebbing. It's fiendish—the more you eat, the more you want.

Red Hot Riplets are pretty ubiquitous. You can find this delicacy at most grocery stores around town, and plenty of restaurants offer them as sides or even include them in their menu items, from burgers and sandwiches to nachos. Red Hot Riplets seasoning is available by itself, so you

can add some of that zing to your own kitchen creations. It's great sprinkled on just about anything, like meat, scrambled eggs, even french fries. I've found it also makes for a mighty tasty rim on my Bloody Mary glass.

BOLYARD'S MEAT & PROVISIONS

2733 Sutton Blvd. | Maplewood | 314.647.2567 | bolyardsmeat.com

Chef Chris Bolyard began his career in the fine-dining world, working for years as the chef de cuisine at Sidney Street Cafe. Eventually he discovered his true calling as a butcher and sausage maker. In 2014 Bolyard left the white tablecloth scene behind and opened Bolyard's Meat & Provisions in Maplewood. The shop moved across the street to its current digs in 2021.

Courtesy of Ryan Reems

There's no shortage of quality butchers in town, but arguably none are as sustainable as Bolyard's. The shop is the only whole-animal butcher in the area, and Bolyard and his crew are very particular about the animals they process. Only those raised on small area farms without confinement and with no hormones or antibiotics will do. The butchering is done in an open room so customers can see exactly what's up. The end result of all of this attention and care includes pretty much any cut imaginable plus sausage, charcuterie, smoked meats, and much more.

But Bolyard's offerings don't stop at meat by the pound. There are also heat-and-eat meals ready for pickup plus house-made stocks and ferments. Catering services include meat platters and boxed lunches. Custom dining experiences held on-site or in-home are also available. Check out the butchering and sausage-making classes routinely held at the shop. Bolyard's has daily lunch service and weekend brunch. In fact, they serve up one of my favorite smash burgers around.

In 2024 Bolyard's took third on *USA Today*'s list of best butchers in the country. Once you visit, you'll wonder how it didn't snag the top spot.

BAETJE FARMS

8932 Jackson School Rd. | Bloomsdale | 573.483.9021 | baetjefarms.com

When I was in the planning stages for this book I decided the spots I focused on would be within the confines of the City of St. Louis or St. Louis County. However, I decided to give Baetje Farms a pass because they're basically just down the road from St. Louis, and their cheeses have become fixtures in the best stores across the metro area.

Baetje Farms has been producing world-renowned goat cheeses in St. Louis's backyard for more than 20 years. Over that time the farm has garnered more than 90 national and international awards for its cheeses. The company was founded in 1998 by Steve and Veronica Baetje. In 2018 it was purchased by an ownership group that includes Cara Naeger and her brothers R.J. Clements and Eric Clements.

Courtesy of Ashleys Portrait Co.

Baetje has plenty of cheeses to choose from, both aged and fresh, and all are handmade. Aged offerings include a couple of Bloomsdale cheeses, named after the area where the farm is located; miette, a bloomy rind goat cheese; and Coeur du Clos, similar to camembert. There are also nine fresh coeur de la crème cheeses available as well as cheese spreads.

So often when original owners pass the torch and sell their business, their vision and passion don't translate to the new guard for a variety of reasons. That's not the case for Baetje. The farm continues to produce the highest-quality French-inspired cheeses. To diversify, the current owners have also introduced a bit of agri-tourism into the mix. The farm now boasts an event space called the Artisan for those interested in a bucolic site for their special function. The property also has some tiny homes available now, so guests can stay on-site and get a true feel for the farm.

ACROSS THE BOARD 314

acrosstheboard314.com

I met Chelsea Foulk, owner of Across the Board 314, by chance while I was interviewing some folks from another business who shared commissary space with her. She told me about her business making custom charcuterie boards and grazing tables, and I was immediately intrigued. I'm always fascinated when someone finds a unique niche and fills it, which is exactly what Foulk has done.

Sometimes the snacks at a soiree are an afterthought, and that's a shame because preprandial bites can make or break a party. Instead of sweaty cubes of Colby Jack, stale pretzels, and warm onion dip, Across the Board 314 takes the highest-quality meats and cheeses and creates spreads that are as visually stunning as they are delicious. In addition to four levels of cheese and charcuterie boards, Foulk also offers full-on grazing tables in three different sizes, a hands-on charcuterie cart experience, crudité platters, and private workshops. There are even catering options for your next corporate shindig or backyard blowout.

Foulk has a background as a cheesemonger and has been in the food and drink game for years, but it was COVID that spurred her to do her own thing. Her passion for what she does is infectious. I challenge anyone to ask Foulk about her creations and not have some of her big cheese energy rub off on them.

I don't just admire Across the Board 314 from afar; I'm also a client. My wife and I ordered a couple of Foulk's creations for a party we threw a while back, and they were a massive hit. Not only were the boards delicious, but Foulk customized them to reflect the theme of the event (sparkles). Plus, it made planning the soiree a whole lot easier. Those boards were almost too pretty to eat. Almost.

Courtesy of Chelsea Foulk

HAWTHORNE HONEY

facebook.com/hawthornehoneystl

I first met Scott Holifield at the Tower Grove Farmers' Market one Saturday morning. I was looking for some honey for a cocktail recipe, and a friend steered me to Holifield's booth with the comment that his Hawthorne Honey was the best around. My friend was not wrong.

Holifield moved to St. Louis for pharmacy school and became entranced by the observation hives at the Missouri Botanical Garden. This inspired him to take a beekeeping class, which further fueled his fascination. Despite his interest, Holifield didn't have the space for hives where he was living at the time. Eventually, though, he and his husband moved to a new neighborhood where he received more encouragement from some beekeeping neighbors. The new place had enough of a backyard that he could start a couple of his own hives.

At first Holifield was more interested in the bees rather than their honey, and he'd give his excess honey to co-workers and friends. They became instant fans, and word spread. Soon enough he began selling to local shops and restaurants, and Hawthorne Honey became a business, named after the street he lives on and the neighborhood's hawthorne trees.

Courtesy of Scott Holfield

Holifield has 20 hives currently, including seven at his home and four on the roof of 21c Museum Hotel downtown, which also uses Hawthorne Honey at its coffee shop, Good Press, and sells it in the hotel gift shop. While he's focused on his own products, which now include creamed honey and hot honey, Holifield also curates varieties from other producers, including orange blossom honey from California and blackberry blossom honey from the Pacific Northwest.

TABERU

taberustl.com

Chef Heidi Skye Hamamura is a triple threat. She's a sushi powerhouse, having learned the craft from her father, sushi master Naomi Hamamura. She cut her teeth in the fine-dining world at highly regarded restaurants like Saint Louis Club and Elaia, so hospitality and attention to every detail are second nature to her. And Hamamura also has a background in visual arts, so her design sense is finely honed. She's taken all of these impressive skills and started Taberu, a private event and catering company that makes stunning savory creations.

Courtesy of Heidi Skye Hamamura

I've always loved sushi. I find the combination of the subtle textures and flavors coupled with the stunning form and colors of the ingredients to be infinitely inspiring. I find even sketchy gas station varieties to be visually arresting (though I'm usually cautious about actually eating it). It's a cuisine that is humble in origin, but Hamamura elevates simple ingredients like rice, seafood, and vegetables into edible artwork that completely transcends the sum of its parts. I liken her handiwork to sand mandalas—beautiful, one of a kind, but ultimately transitory. Hamamura is all about omakase. The word translates to "trust the chef." Just give her some basic info like allergies and any flavors that are totally off limits, and let her imagination run free.

Taberu creations can also be experienced at pop-up dinners around town and events like the Japanese Festival at the Missouri Botanical Garden, held every Labor Day weekend, and the Red Lantern City Night Market in the Central

West End each summer, which Hamamura founded in 2020. Taberu also offers in-home sushi classes, full sushi dining experiences for groups of various sizes, and large-scale catering for events like weddings and parties. Want to show someone how much you love them? Order one of Taberu's crazy sushi cakes. You'll never order a sad grocery store sheet cake again.

Courtesy of Heidi Skye Hamamura

INDEX